The Ship of Salvation

Safīnat al-najā

The Doctrine and Jurisprudence of the School of al-Imām al-Shāfii

A classic manual of Islāmic Doctrine and Jurisprudence In Arabic with English text, commentary and appendices

Sālim ibn ʿAbdullah ibn Saʿd ibn Samīr al-Haḍramī al-Shāfiʿī

Translated by

ʿAbdullah Muḥammad al-Marbūqī al-Shāfiʿi

سفينة النجاء

بسم الله الرحمن الرحيم

Indeed Allah ﷻ Has Intelligent Servants,

Who Have Divorced the World and Who Fear Temptations,

They Pondered in the World and When They Knew,

That it is Not a Homeland for a Living Person,

They Took it as a Deep Sea and They Made,

Good Actions in the World Their ***Ships.***

Contents

Transliteration Key

ا	a	ر	r	ف	f
ب	b	ز	z	ق	q
ت	t	س	s	ك	k
ث	th	ش	sh	ل	l
ج	j	ص	ṣ	م	m
ح	ḥ	ض	ḍ	ن	n
خ	kh	ط	ṭ	و	w
د	d	ظ	ẓ	ه	h
ذ	dh	غ	gh	ي	y

Long wovels		Short wovels	
ا	ā	ـَ	a
ي	ī	ـِ	i
و	ū	ـُ	u
Diphtong		**Doubled**	
ـَو	aw	ـُوَّ	uwwa
ـَي	ay	ـِيَّ	iyya

The letter *hamzah* "ء" is transliterated as a right half ring (ʾ) and is not expressed when at the beginning.
The letter ʿ*ayn* "ع" is transliterated as a left half ring (ʿ).
ـة is transliterated as "*ah*" in pause form and "*at*" in construct form.
ال is transliterated as "*al*" in both; pause and construct form, "*al*" is used with all letters; *hurūf al-shamsiyyah* or *hurūf al-qamariyyah.*

Honorific

سبحانه وتعالى Glorified and Most High.
ﷺ May Allah's blessings and peace be upon him.
عليه السلام May peace be upon him.
رضي الله عنه May Allah be pleased with him/her.
رضي الله عنهم May Allah be pleased with them

Translator's Preface

الحمد لله رب العالمين ، والصلاة والسلام على عبده ورسوله محمد وآله وصحبه أجمعين . أما بعد .

In the name of Allah, the Merciful, the Compassionate.

All praise is to Allah, the Lord of all the worlds. Peace and blessings be upon His noble Slave and Messenger, Muḥammad and upon his family and Companions.

وعَنْ أَمِيرِ الْمُؤمِنِينَ أَبِى حَفْصٍ عُمَرَ بْنِ الخَطَّابِ ﵁ قَالَ: سَمِعْتُ رَسُولَ اللّٰهِ ﷺ يَقُولُ: **«إِنَّمَا الأَعْمَالُ بِالنِّيَّاتِ وَإِنَّمَا لِكُلِّ امْرِئٍ مَا نَوَى ، فَمَنْ كَانَتْ هِجْرَتُهُ إِلَى اللّٰهِ وَرَسُولِهِ فَهِجْرَتُهُ إِلَى اللّٰهِ وَرَسُولِهِ ، وَمَنْ كَانَتْ هِجْرَتُهُ إِلَى دُنْيَا يُصِيبُهَا وَ امْرَأَةٍ يَنْكِحُهَا فَهِجْرَتُهُ إِلَى مَا هَاجَرَ إِلَيْهِ»** (متفق عليه).

Amīr al-Muʾminīn Abū Ḥafs Sayyidunā ʿUmar ibn al-Khaṭṭab ﵁ narrated that he heard Rasūlullah ﷺ saying, "Verily the reward for deeds depend upon intentions and indeed every person shall receive what he intended for. Thus, he whose emigration was for Allah and His Messenger, his emigration will be considered for Allah and His Messenger. He whose emigration was towards the world or to be married to a woman, his emigration will be for whatever he migrated for."

This book has been prepared for the beginner, especially those students studying at a "madrasah". Many Arabic terminologies have been maintained with the translation in the bracket.

Footnotes provide assistance for teacher in explaining the text. The students are required to be familiar with the text of *Safīnat al-najā'*. It is better if the students can memorize the Arabic text so that they gain acquaintance with the jurisprudence or at least be able to read it fluently.

Every effort was made to present a precise and accurate translation with proper explanations. The explanations were mostly derived from "*Kāshifat al-sajā' sharh Safīnat al-najā'*", "Reliance of the Traveller" and "*al-Iqnā' fī halli alfāẓi matn Abī Shujā'*". The additional chapter of Ḥajj and 'Umrah was taken from the "*Al-Fiqh al-manhaji 'alā madhhab al-Imām al-Shāfi'ī,*" and "Reliance of the Traveller".The measurements and conversions were based on the book, "*al-Maqādīr al-shar'iyyah*" by Dr. Najm al-dīn al-Kurdī. The biographical notes were taken from the book, "Reliance of the Traveller".

I would like to take this opportunity to pay a particular tribute to my mother. It is through her sacrifice and du'ā that I was able to reach this stage. It is incumbent upon me to extend my deepest gratitude to my elders: Muftī Ibrahīm Desai and Mawlānā Muḥammad Ṭaha Karan for their encouragement and support.

This work is completed with the tremendous help and assistant of my ustadh, Mawlānā Muḥammad ibn Harun 'Abasoomar, my brother Hāfiẓ Luqmān Hasbi, my friends Hāfiẓ Reeaz Iqbal and Hāfiẓ Ziyād Danka. This book could not have been published without significant aid from Mawlānā Ibrahim Muḥammad and Mawlānā Imran Hatia. May Allah ﷻ reward them and all those who were involved directly or indirectly in completing this task, here and in the hereafter.

Lastly, I beseech Almighty Allah ﷻ for His acceptance and that He ﷻ makes this a source of benefit for all. Āmīn.

'Abdullah Muḥammad al-Marbūqī al-Shāfi'ī
Shah Alam, Selangor
Ṣafar 1430 H

سفينة النجاء

□ أ□□□راهـ □ □رإيسـ

□ل□ م هسب الإما□ر□افع □

The Ship of Salvation

The Doctrine and Jurisprudence
of the School of al-Imām al-Shāfiʿī

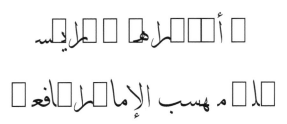

Muqaddimah

« مَنْ يُرِدِ اللّـــهُ بِهِ خَيْراً يُفَقِّهْهُ فِي الدِّينِ » (البخاري)

For whomsoever Allah ﷻ intends goodness, He gives him the understanding of Dīn. [al-Bukhārī]

بِسْمِ اللّـــهِ الرَّحْمٰنِ الرَّحِيْمِ

الْحَمْدُ لِلّـــهِ رَبِّ الْعَالَمِينَ وَبِهِ نَسْتَعِينُ عَلَى أُمُورِ الدُّنْيَا وَالدِّينِ وَصَلَّى اللّـــهُ وَسَلَّمَ عَلَى سَيِّدِنَا مُحَمَّدٍ خَاتَمِ النَّبِيِّينَ وَآلِهِ وَصَحْبِهِ أَجْمَعِينَ وَلاَ حَوْلَ وَلاَ قُوَّةَ إِلاَّ بِاللّـــهِ الْعَلِيِّ الْعَظِيمِ.

In the name of Allah, the Merciful, the Compassionate.

All praise is to Allah, the Lord of all the worlds. We seek help from Him in worldly affairs and in matters of Dīn. Salutation and peace on our Master, Muḥammad ﷺ, the Seal of Prophethood, and upon all his family and Companions. There is no power and might except through Allah, the Most High, the Most Great.

Islam and Iman

Islam and Iman

فصل : أَرْكَانُ الإِسْلامِ خَمْسَةٌ :

(1) شَهَادَةُ أَنْ لا إِلَهَ إِلاَّ اللّٰهُ وَأَنَّ مُحَمَّدًا رَسُولُ اللّٰهِ (2) وَإِقَامُ الصَّلاةِ (3)

وَإِيتَاءُ الزَّكَاةِ (4) وَصَوْمُ رَمَضَانَ (5) وَحِجُّ الْبَيْتِ مَنِ اسْتَطَاعَ إِلَيْهِ سَبِيلا.

Section: The Integrals of Islām are Five:

1. To bear witness that there is no god except Allah and that Muḥammad ﷺ is the messenger of Allah.
2. To establish ṣalāh.[1]
3. To discharge zakāh.[2]
4. To fast in the month of Ramaḍān.[3]
5. To perform ḥajj for those who are able.[4]

---

[1] The most virtuous physical worship is ṣalāh, then fasting, then ḥajj and then zakāh. As for worship pertaining to the heart like *imān* (belief), *ma'rifah* (gnosis), *tafakkur* (reflection), trust in Allah ﷻ, patience, hope, contentment with Allah's decree, love of Allah ﷻ, repentance, purification of blameworthy traits like greed, anger, pride, malice etc. these are far more superior than physical worship. The most virtuous of them being *īmān*.

[2] Zakāh literally means growth, blessings, purification or praise. In Sacred Law it is the name for a particular amount of property that must be paid to certain kinds of recipients under certain conditions.

[3] Fasting was made farḍ in Sha'bān, the second year Hijrī. Rasulullah ﷺ fasted for nine complete Ramaḍāns.

[4] Both ḥajj and 'umrah are wājib in the Shāfi'ī's madhhab (school of thought).

فصل : أَرْكَانُ الإِيمَانِ سِتَّةٌ :

(1) أَنْ تُؤْمِنَ بِاللَّـــهِ (2) وَمَلائِكَتِهِ (3) وَكُتُبِهِ (4) وَرُسُلِهِ (5) وَبِالْيَوْمِ الآخِرِ

(6) وَبِالْقَدَرِ خَيْرِهِ وَشَرِّهِ مِنَ اللَّــهِ تَعَالَى .

Section: The Integrals of Īmān (Faith) are Six:

1. To believe in Allah.[5]
2. To believe in His Angels.[6]
3. To believe in His Books.[7]

---

[5] **[Īmān *Mujmāl* (in brief)]** To believe in Allah's ﷻ existence, His sole godhood, that no one else participates in His attribute of divinity or in the rights He has over His creation, His oneness and uniqueness and that He is characterized by every perfection and exalted above any imperfection or impossibility. **[Īmān *Mufaṣṣal* (in detail)]** It is wājib to know the attributes of Allah ﷻ: (1) *al-Wujūd* (Being), (2) *al-Qidām* (Pre-eternity), (3) *al-Baqā'* (Everlastingness), (4) *Mukhālafatuh ta'āla bi al-hawādith* (Absolute dissimilarity to created things), (5) *Qiyāmuh ta'āla bī nafsih* (Self-subsistence), (6) *al-Wahdāniyah* (Oneness), (7) *al-Qudrah* (Power), (8) *al-Irādah* (Will), (9) *al-'Ilm* (Knowledge), (10) *al-Hayāh* (Life) (11) *al-Sam'* (Hearing), (12) *al-Baṣr* (Sight), (13) *al-Kalām* (Speech).

[6] To believe that the Angels are the honourable servants of Allah ﷻ, who do not disobey Him and do as they are commanded. They are created from light, not characterized by gender, neither male nor female, nor do they eat or drink. It is wājib to know ten of them: (1) ***Jibrīl***, (2) ***Mīkā'īl***, (3) ***Isrāfīl***, (4) ***'Izrā'īl***, (5) ***Munkar***, (6) ***Nakīr***, (7) ***Riḍwān***, (8) ***Mālik***, (9) ***Raqīb***, and (10) ***'Ā tīd***.

[7] To believe in all the Books revealed by Allah to His messengers. It is wājib to know four books in particular: (1) the ***Tawrah*** of Nabī Mūsā

4. To believe in His Messengers.[8]

5. To believe in the Final Day.[9]

6. To believe in Destiny, good and evil, is from Allah the Exalted.[10]

[img], (2) the **Zabur** of Nabī Dāwud [img], (3) the *Injīl* of Nabī ʿĪsā [img] and (4) the **Qurʾān** of Nabī Muhammad [img].

[8] To believe in the Prophets and Messengers of Allah [img], that Allah [img] sent them to man and jinn to guide them to the path of the Truth. Four attributes are necessary for all Messengers (1) Truthfullness, (2) Trustworthiness, (3) Conveying the message, and (4) Intelligence. It is wājib to know twenty-five of them: (1) *Adām*, (2) *Idrīs* (Enoch), (3) *Nūh* (Noah), (4) *Hūd*, (5) *Ṣalīh*, (6) *Lūṭ* (Lot), (7) *Ibrāhīm* (Abraham), (8) *Ismāʿīl* (Ishmael), (9) *Ishāq* (Isaac), (10) *Yaʿqūb* (Jacob), (11) *Yūsuf* (Joseph), (12) *Shūʿaib*, (13) *Ayyūb* (Job), (14) *Dhul Kiflī* (Ezekiel), (15) *Mūsā* (Moses), (16) *Hārūn* (Aaron), (17) *Dāwud* (David), (18) *Sūlaymān* (Soloman), (19) *Ilyās* (Elias), (20) *al-Yāsaʿ* (Elisha), (21) *Yūnus* (Jonah), (22) *Zakariyyā* (Zacharias), (23) *Yahyā* (John), (24) *ʿĪsā* (Jesus), and (25) **Muḥammad** (Peace and Salutation upon him and upon all of them).

[9] To believe that everyone will die, and will then be resurrected. It also means to believe without doubt in *Jannah* (Heaven) and *Jahannam* (Hell), the *Mīzān* (Scale), the *Ṣirāṭ* (Path - the bridge over the Fire), the Questioning in the grave, the Reckoning (after the Resurrection), the Recompense (in Paradise), Punishment (for some sinful believers) and Torment (eternal for the unbeliever). Some will be put in Hell out of justice and some in Paradise out of Allah's sheer generosity.

[10] To believe that Allah [img] has ordained both good and evil before creating the creation and that all that has been and all that will be exists only through Allah's *Qaḍāʾ* (Decree), *Qadr* (Foreordinance) and *Irādah* (Will).

فصل : وَمَعْنَى لا إِلَهَ إِلاَّ اللَّــهُ لا مَعْبُودَ بِحَقٍّ فِي الْوُجُودِ إِلاَّ اللَّــهُ .

Section: The meaning of the Kalimah is “In reality none is worthy of worship except Allah”.

Al-Ahkam al-Shar' iyyah

Note: *Al-Ahkam al-Shar'iyyah* - The Rulings of the Sacred Law:

In the Shāfi'ī Madhhab (school of thought), the actions of those who are obligated to observe the precepts of religion take one of five rulings:

1. The *Wājib* (obligatory) action: One will be rewarded for performing them and will be liable for punishment upon abandoning them.
2. The *Mandūb* (recommended) action: One will be rewarded for performing them and will not be liable for punishment upon abandoning them.
3. The *Mubāḥ* (permissible) action: One will not be rewarded for performing them and will not be liable for punishment upon abandoning them.
4. The *Makrūh* (offensive) action: One will be rewarded for abandoning them and will not be liable for punishment upon performing them.
5. The *Ḥarām* (forbidden) action: One will be rewarded for abandoning them and will be liable for punishment upon performing them.

Taharah

Taharah

فصل : عَلامَاتُ الْبُلُوغِ ثَلاثٌ :

(1) تَمَامُ خَمْسَ عَشْرَةَ سَنَةً فِي الذَّكَرِ وَالأُنثَى (2) وَالاحْتِلامُ فِي الذَّكَرِ وَالأُنثَى لِتِسْعِ سِنِينَ (3) وَالْحَيْضُ فِي الأُنثَى لِتِسْعِ سِنِينَ .

Section: The Signs of Puberty are Three:[1]

1. Reaching the age of 15 (lunar) years for a male or a female.
2. Experiencing a wet dream by a 9 year old boy or girl.
3. Menstruation for a 9 year old girl.[2]

---

[1] When a child reaches the age of seven and is *mumayyiz* (discerning) i.e. he can eat, drink and clean himself after using the toilet unassisted, he is ordered to perform ṣalāh and all other injunctions pertaining to ṣalāh (e.g. wuḍū'). When he reaches ten, he will be beaten for neglecting it, not severely, but so as to discipline the child, and not more than three strikes. ṣalāh and other injuctions of Sharīʿah become wājib when a child reaches the age of puberty.

[2] Pregnancy is not a sign of puberty, rather an emission of sexual fluid prior to pregnancy is.

فصل : شُرُوطُ إِجْزَاءِ الْحَجَرِ ثَمَانِيَةٌ :

(1) أَنْ يَكُونَ بِثَلَاثَةِ أَحْجَارٍ (2) وَأَنْ يُنْقِيَ الْـمَحَلَّ (3) وَأَنْ لا يَجفَّ النَّجَسُ

(4) وَلا يَنْتَقِلَ (5) وَلا يَطْرَأَ عَلَيْهِ آخرُ (6) وَلا يُجَاوِزَ صَفْحَتَهُ وَحَشَفَتَهُ (7)

وَلا يُصِيبَهُ مَاءٌ (8) وَأَنْ تَكُونَ الأَحْجَارُ طَاهِرَةً .

Section: The Conditions for Using a Stone[3] (to clean the private parts) are Eight:[4]

1. Three[5] stones should be used.[6]
2. It should purify.[7]
3. The impurity should not be completely dry.[8]
4. The impurity should not have spread out.[9]
5. No other impurity should come upon it.

[3] Stones suffice to clean oneself, though it is best to follow this up by washing with water.
[4] It is wājib to use water if one of these conditions is not found.
[5] It is wājib to use either three stones or even three sides of one stone when one is sufficient to remove impurities. Otherwise one needs to repeat using a stone that suffices in removing the impurity. It is sunnah to use an odd number of stones (meaning three, five, seven etc.).
[6] Anything that is solid, pure and removes filth. Something deserving respect (e.g. paper; an instrument of knowledge) or something edible can not replace the use of stones.
[7] It means to remove the filth so that nothing remains but a trace that could not be removed unless one were to use water. When this has been done, any remaining effect of impurity is excusable.
[8] If the impurity becomes dry, using a stone will no longer suffice.
[9] Impurity should not reach another part of the body.

6. The impurity should not go beyond the inner buttock[10] and the head of the penis.
7. Water should not splash onto the stone.[11]
8. The stones to be used should be pure.

Note: The Sunnah Way for Using a Stone:

1. Begin to wipe from front to back on the right side with the first stone, similarly wipe the left with the second, and wipe both sides and the anus with the third. Each wiping must begin at a point on the skin that is free of impurity.
2. It is sunnah (recommended) to add an odd number of stones e.g. five, seven and so on.
3. It is makrūh (offensive) to use the right hand to clean the impurity.

---

[10] Inner buttock refers to that which is enfolded when standing.
[11] It will not be valid to use a wet stone.

فصل : فُرُوضُ الوُضُوءِ سِتَّةٌ :

الأَوَّلُ النِّـــيَّـــةُ **الثَّاني** غَسْلُ الْوَجْهِ **الثَّالِثُ** غَسْلُ الْيَدَيْنِ مَعَ المِرْفَقَيْنِ **الرَّابِـــعُ** مَسْحُ شَيْءٍ مِنَ الرَّأْسِ **الْـــخَامِسُ** غَسْلُ الرِّجْلَيْنِ مَعَ الْكَعْبَيْنِ **السَّادِسُ** التَّرتِيبُ .

Section: The Obligatory Acts of Wuḍū᾽ (Ritual Ablution) are Six:

1. Intention.[12]
2. Washing the face.[13]
3. Washing both hands and arms including the elbows.[14]
4. Wiping any part of the head.[15]
5. Washing the feet including the ankles.
6. *Tartīb* (to observe the above-mentioned sequence).

فصل : النِّـــيَّـــةُ قَصْدُ الشَّيْءِ مُقْتَرِناً بِفِعْلِهِ وَمَحَلُّهَا القَلْبُ وَالتَّلَفُّظُ بِهَا سُنَّةٌ وَوَقْتُهَا عِنْدَ غَسْلِ أَوَّلِ جُزْءٍ مِنَ الْوَجْهِ والتَّرْتِيبُ أَنْ لا يُقَدَّمَ عُضْوٌ عَلَى عُضْوٍ .

---

[12] The person performing ablution either intends removing a state of *ḥadath* (ritual impurity) or purification for the ṣalāh.

[13] Washing the entire face, from the point where the hairline usually begins to the chin in length, and from ear to ear in width.

[14] Washing both arms completely, up-to and including the elbows once.

[15] The minimum is to wipe part of a single hair, provided this part does not hang below the limit of the head (i.e. below the hairline).

Section: Intention is to intend something simultaneously with the action; its place is in the heart. To make a verbal intention is a sunnah; its time is at the beginning of washing the first portion of the face. *Tartīb* (sequence) is to observe the sequence of the wuḍū', such that no latter limb of wuḍū' should precede a former limb.

Note: The Sunnah Way to Perform Wuḍū' (Ritual Ablution):

1. Recite *ta'awwudh*: I take refuge in Allah from the accursed Shaitan (to recite *A'udhubillah* completely), and *basmalah*: In the name of Allah, Most Merciful, Most Compassionate (to recite *Bismillah* completely).
2. Wash the hands up-to and including the wrists three times.
3. Use the *miswāk* (toothstick), and then rinse the mouth and nose out three times, with three handfuls of water. One takes in a mouthful from a handful of water and snifts up some of the rest of the handful into the nostrils thrice.
4. Wash the entire face, from the point where the hairline usually begins to the chin in length, and from ear to ear in width, three times. It is obligatory to wash all facial hair – inner, outer, as well as the skin beneath the hair, whether the hair is thick or thin – such as the eyebrows, moustache and so forth except for a thick beard.

5. Wash both arms completely, up-to and including the elbows, three times. It is sunnah to pass the fingers through each other.
6. Wipe the head by passing the wet hands from the front of the head, sliding the paired hands to the back up to the nape of the neck, and then return them to point of commencement, three times.
7. Wipe the inside of the ears with the fingertips and their outside with the thumbs, with fresh water, three times.
8. Wash the feet up-to and including the ankles, three times. Allow the water to pass between the toes by using the little finger of the left hand, beginning with the little toe of the right foot, and ending with the little toe on the left.
9. During wuḍū᾽, it is sunnah:

   - to wash the limbs successively,

   - to begin with the right when washing the arms and legs, but both hands, cheeks, or ears, are washed simultaneously,

   - to begin with the top of the face and not to splash the water onto it,

   - to avoid splashing water onto oneself,

   - to face the qiblah, not to talk except for a necessity, and

   - not to waste water.

Note: The Cleanliness of the Body:

It is sunnah (1) to trim the fingernails and toenails, (2) to clip moustache to the extent that the pink of the upper lip is visible, it should not be plucked or shaved, (3) to pluck (or to shave) the hair of the underarms and nostrils, and to shave the pubic hair (4) to apply kuhl (an antimonic compound), (5) to apply henna for women.

Circumcision is wājib for both men and women.

It is ḥarām for both; men and women to dye their hair black, except with the intention of jihād.

فصل : الماءُ قَلِيلٌ وَكَثِيرٌ : الْقَلِيلُ مَا دُونَ الْقُلَّتَيْنِ . وَالْكَثِيرُ قُلَّتَانِ فَأَكْثَرُ الْقَلِيلُ يَتَنَجَّسُ بِوُقُوعِ النَّجَاسَةِ فِيهِ وَإِنْ لَمْ يَتَغَيَّرْ وَالْـــمَاءُ الْكَثِيرُ لَا يَتَنَجَّسُ إِلاَّ إِذَا تَغَيَّرَ طَعْمُهُ أَوْ لَوْنُهُ أَوْ رِيُحُهُ .

Section: Water[16] is Either a Little or Abundant.[17]

* A little amount of water is that which is less than two *qullahs*.

---

[16] The definition of *mā' al-mutlaq* (general water) is that water which is without any attributes.

[17] It is not permissible to remove hadath (wuḍū' or ritual bath) or remove impurity except with "general water".

- Abundant water that which is two *qullahs* (approximately 190 litres) or more.
- A little amount of water will become impure when any impurity[18] falls into it, even though the water does not change.[19]
- Abundant water will not become impure except when its taste, colour or smell changes.

فصل : مُوجِبَاتُ الْغُسْلِ سِتَّةٌ :

(1) إِيلاجُ الْحَشَفَةِ فِي الْفَرْجِ (2) وَخُرُوجُ الْمَنِيِّ (3) وَالْحَيْضُ (4) وَالنِّفَاسُ (5) وَالْوِلادَةُ (6) وَالْمَوْتُ .

Section: The Things Make a Ritual Bath Compulsory are Six:

1. Insertion the head of the penis into the vagina.[20]
2. Discharge of semen.[21]

---

[18] If an impurity which is so small (e.g. impurity on the leg of a fly) that it is indiscernible by eyesight (meaning an average look that is neither a negligent glance nor a detailed inspection) or a dead creature without flowing blood falls into it, in both cases the water remains purifying. This applies to both running or stagnant water.

[19] Even though none of the water's characteristics (i.e. taste, colour or smell) have changed.

[20] Insertion of the head of the penis into the front or back private part of a male or female human, or animal, adult or minor, living or dead, will necessitate a ritual bath.

3. Menstruation.[22]
4. Postnatal bleeding.[23]
5. Childbirth.[24]
6. Death.[25]

فصل : فُرُوضُ الغُسْلِ اثْنَانِ :

(1) النِّـــيَّـــةُ (2) وَتَعْمِيمُ الْبَدَنِ بِالْـــمَاءِ .

Section: The Compulsory Acts of a Ritual Bath are Two:

1. Intention.[26]
2. To ensure that water reaches the entire body.[27]

---

[21] Male sperm and female sexual fluid are recognized by the fact that they (1) come in spurts by contractions, (2) with sexual gratification and (3) when moist, smell like bread dough, and when dry, like egg-white.

[22] Periodic discharge of blood from the vagina.

[23] Blood discharged after giving birth.

[24] Ritual bath becomes wājib even in the case of dry birth or miscarriage.

[25] It is wājib to give a bath to a Muslim who is non-martyr. It is not wājib to give a bath to a disbeliever, though it is permissible. It is ḥarām to give a bath and to offer ṣalāh upon a martyr.

[26] The intention is of removing *hadath* or *janābah* (major ritual impurity) or removing the impurity of haiḍ (menstruation). One bath will suffice with the intention of removing both major ritual impurity and the sunnah of the Friday prayer, though if only one intention is made, the bath counts for that one but not the other.

[27] The water reaches all of the hair and skin, to the roots of the hair, under the nails and the outwardly visible portion of the ear canals, including the area under the foreskin of an uncircumcized man, and the

Note: The Sunnah Way to Perform a Ritual Bath:

4. To begin in the name of Allah, the Merciful, the Compassionate (to recite *Bismillah* completely).
5. To remove any dirt or impurity on the body.
6. To perform wuḍū᾽ as the wuḍū᾽ of ṣalāh.
7. To pour water over the head three times intending to remove a major hadath (ritual impurity) or haiḍ (menstruation).
8. To pour water over the right side of the body three times and then left side three times, ensuring that water reaches all joints and folds, and to rub oneself.
9. It is sunnah to apply musk (or any other fragrance) on a piece of cotton and insert it into the vagina if the bath was taken because of haiḍ.

فصل : شُرُوط الوُضُوءِ عَشَرَةٌ :

(1) الإِسْلامُ (2) وَالتَّمْيِيزُ (3) وَالنَّــقَاءُ عَنِ الْحَيْضِ وَالنِّفَاسِ (4) وَعَمّا يَمْنَعُ وُصُولَ الــمَاءِ إِلَى الْبَشَرَةِ (5) وَأَنْ لا يَكُونَ عَلَى الْعُضْوِ مَا يُغَيِّرُ الــمَاءَ (6)

---

private part of a non-virgin woman which is normally exposed when she squats to relieve herself.

وَالْعِلْمُ بِفَرْضِيَّتِهِ (7) وَأَنْ لا يَعْتَقِدَ فَرْضاً مِنْ فُرُوضِهِ سُنَّةً (8) وَالْمَاءُ الطَّهُورُ

(9) وَدُخُولُ الْوَقْتِ (10) وَالْمُوَالاةُ لِدَائِمِ الْحَدَثِ .

Section: The Conditions of Wuḍū' are Ten:[28]

1. Islām .
2. The age of understanding.[29]
3. Cleanliness from menstruation and postnatal bleeding.
4. Being free from that which prevents the water from reaching the skin.
5. Nothing should be upon the limb that will change the (qualities of the) water.
6. Knowledge of it (wuḍū') being obligatory.
7. Not to assume the farḍ (obligatory) acts as sunnah (recommended).[30]
8. Pure water.
9. – 10. Entering of the time (of ṣalāh)[31] and Continuity, for a person who constantly remains in the state of impurity.

---

[28] The conditions for the validity of wuḍū', these conditions are also applied for a ritual bath.
[29] A child reaches the stage of mumayyiz (discerning) when he can eat, drink and clean himself after using the toilet unassisted.
[30] For the general public, it is suffice to know some of its acts are farḍ and some are sunnah.
[31] Wuḍū' or a ritual bath should be performed after the entering of the ṣalāhs' time for farḍ ṣalāh or at a particular time for sunnah ṣalāh (e.g. dhuhā).

فصل : نَوَاقِضُ الْوُضُوءِ أَرْبَعَةُ أَشْيَاءَ :

الأَوَّلُ الْخَارِجُ مِنْ أَحَدِ السَّبِيلَيْنِ مِنْ قُبُلٍ أَوْ دُبُرٍ رِيحٌ أَوْ غَيْرُهُ إِلاَّ الْـمَنِيَّ **الثَّانِي** زَوَالُ الْعَقْلِ بِنَومٍ أَوْ غَيْرِهِ إِلاَّ نَوْمَ قَاعِدٍ مُمَكِّنٍ مَقْعَدَهُ مِنَ الْأَرْضِ **الثَّالِثُ** الْتِقَاءُ بَشَرَتَيْ رَجُلٍ وَامْرَأَةٍ كَبِيرَيْنِ أَجْنَبِيَّيْنِ مِنْ غَيْرِ حَائِلٍ **الرَّابِعُ** مَسُّ قُبُلِ الآدَمِيِّ أَوْ حَلْقَةِ دُبُرِهِ بِبَطْنِ الرَّاحَةِ أَوْ بُطُونِ الأَصَابِعِ.

Section: The Factors that Nullify the Wuḍūʾ are Four:

1. Anything that exits from either the front or the rear private parts, whether wind or anything else,[32] except semen.[33]
2. Loss of intellect[34] through sleep or other causes,[35] except sleep while firmly seated on the ground.
3. Skin-to-skin contact between an adult,[36] non-mahram (marriageable), male and female without any barrier.[37]

---

[32] Or anything else whether common or uncommon such as a worm or stone but not *manī* (semen).

[33] An example of this being someone firmly seated who sleeps and has a wet dream, or someone who looks at something lustfully and sperm or sexual fluid are emitted.

[34] Meaning the loss of the ability to distinguish.

[35] Or other causes like insanity, drunkenness etc. excludes drowsing and daydreaming, which do not break wuḍūʾ. Among the signs of drowsing is that one can hear the words of those present, even though without comprehension.

[36] Adult means the age that usually stirs up sexual desire in a person. Wuḍūʾ will not break if this is only found in one of the two.

4. Touching the private parts of a human with the palm or inner surface of the fingers.[38]

فَصْلٌ : مَنِ انْتَقَضَ وُضُوءُهُ حَرُمَ عَلَيْهِ أَرْبَعَةُ أَشْيَاءَ :

(1) الصَّلَاةُ (2) وَالطَّوَافُ (3) وَمَسُّ الْـمُصْحَفِ (4) وَحَمْلُهُ .

وَيَحْرُمُ عَلَى الْجُنُبِ سِتَّةُ أَشْيَاءَ :

(1) الصَّلَاةُ (2) وَالطَّوَافُ (3) وَمَسُّ الْـمُصْحَفِ (4) وَحَمْلُهُ (5) وَاللُّبْثُ فِي الْـمَسْجِدِ (6) وَقِرَاءَةُ الْقُرْآنِ .

وَيَحْرُمُ بِالْحَيْضِ عَشَرَةُ أَشْيَاءَ :

(1) الصَّلَاةُ (2) وَالطَّوَافُ (3) وَمَسُّ الْـمُصْحَفِ (4) وَحَمْلُهُ (5) وَاللُّبْثُ فِي الْـمَسْجِدِ (6) وَقِرَاءَةُ الْقُرْآنِ (7) وَالصَّوْمُ (8) وَالطَّلَاقُ (9) وَالْـمُرُورُ فِي الْـمَسْجِدِ إِنْ خَافَتْ تَلْوِيثَهُ (10) وَالِاسْتِمْتَاعُ بِمَا بَيْنَ السُّرَّةِ وَالرُّكْبَةِ .

---

[37] The wuḍū' will break even if they touch without sexual desire, or unintentionally, and even if be with the tongue or a malfunctional surplus limb. Touching does not include contact with teeth, nails, hair or a severed limb. Wuḍū' is also broken by touching an aged person or a corpse of the opposite sex.

[38] Those parts of the palm which touch each-other when the hands are put together palm to palm.

Section:

The Forbidden Actions for a Person in the State of Minor Impurity (in need of wuḍū᾽) are Four:

(1) Ṣalāh, (2) ṭawāf, (3) touching or (4) carrying the Qur᾽ān.[39]

The Forbidden Actions for a Person in the State of Major Impurity (in Need of Ritual Bath) are Six:

(1) Ṣalah, (2) ṭawāf, (3) touching, (4) carrying or (5) reciting the Qur᾽ān and (6) to remain in the masjid.

The Forbidden Actions for a Person in the State of Menstruation are Ten:

(1) Salat, (2) ṭawāf, (3) touching or, (4) carrying the Qur᾽ān, (5) to remain in the masjid, (6) reciting the Qur᾽ān, (7) fasting, (8) divorce, (9) to pass through the masjid for a woman who thinks her blood might soil the masjid, and (10) to take sexual pleasure from what is between the navel and the knees.

فصل : أَسْبَابُ التَّيَمُّمِ ثَلاثَةٌ :

(1) فَقْدُ الْـــمَاءِ (2) وَالمــَــرَضُ (3) وَالاحْتِيَاجُ إِلَيْهِ لِعَطَشِ حَيَوَانٍ مُحْتَرَمٍ .

وَغَيْرُ الْـــمُحْتَرَمِ سِتَّةٌ :

---

[39] It is not permissible to touch the Qur᾽ān, whether its writing, the spaces between its lines, its margins, binding, the carrying strap attached to it, or the bag or box it is in. However, it is permissible to carry a Qur᾽ān in baggage and to carry money, rings, or clothes on which Qur᾽ān is written.

(1) تَارِكُ الصَّلَاةِ (2) وَالزَّانِي الْـمُحْصَنُ (3) وَالْـمُرْتَدُّ (4) وَالْكَافِرُ الْحَرْبِيُّ

(5) وَالْكَلْبُ الْعَقُورُ (6) وَالْخِنْـزِيرُ .

Section: The Causes of Tayammum (Dry Ablution) are Three:

1. Absence of water.[40]
2. Illness.[41]
3. Need for water exists by (oneself or) worthy animals.[42]

   The following six people or animals are classified unworthy:

   1. A person who forsakes ṣalāh.
   2. A convicted married adulterer.
   3. An Apostate.
   4. A non-Muslim from a non-Muslim country that has war with the Muslim country.
   5. A vicious dog.
   6. A pig.

---

[40] If there is a little water that is insufficient for attaining purity, water should be used as much as possible and then tayammum should be performed for the rest of the limbs.

[41] An ailment that a person fears water would cause, (1) harm to life or limb, (2) disability, (3) becoming seriously ill, (4) an increase in one's ailment, (5) a delay in recovering from one's illness, (6) considerable pain, or (7) a bad effect from the water such as a radical change in one's skin colour or a visible part of the body.

[42] There is fear of one's own thirst, or that of worthy companions and animals with one, even if be in the future.

فصل : شُرُوطُ التَّيَمُّمِ عَشَرَةٌ :

(1) أَنْ يَكُونَ بِتُرَابٍ (2) وَأَنْ يَكُونَ التُّرَابُ طَاهِرًا (3) وَأَنْ لا يَكُونَ مُسْتَعْمَلا (4) وَأَنْ لا يُخَالِطُهُ دَقِيقٌ وَنَحْوُهُ (5) وَأَنْ يَقْصِدَهُ (6) وَأَنْ يَمْسَحَ وَجْهَهُ وَيَدَيْهِ بِضَرْبَتَيْنِ (7) وَأَنْ يُزِيلَ النَّجَاسَةَ أَوَّلا (8) وَأَنْ يَجْتَهِدَ فِي القِبْلَةِ قَبْلَهُ (9) وَأَنْ يَكُوْنَ التَّيَمُّمُ بَعْدَ دُخُولِ الْوَقْتِ (10) وَأَنْ يَتَيَمَّمَ لِكُلِّ فَرْضٍ .

Section: The Conditions of Tayammum are Ten:

1. It must be performed with (dust of) the earth.[43]
2. The dust must be pure.
3. The dust must not be used (i.e. already used on a limb or has been dusted off a limb).
4. The dust must not be mixed with flour or anything like flour.[44]
5. A person should intend the earth.[45]
6. He should wipe his face and both hands with two strikes of dust.

---

[43] It does not matter whether the earth is red, black, yellow or salty in which nothing grows. It is not permissible to perform tayammum with earth that has been turned to ashes or with clay pottery that has been pounded and softened.

[44] Like saffron or lime.

[45] Therefore, if the wind blew earth onto a person and one then passed one's hands over one's face and arms, the tayammum will not be valid even though one stood in the wind with intention of having sand blown over one.

7. He should first remove any impurity.
8. He should determine the direction of the qiblah before commencing the tayammum.[46]
9. He should make tayammum after the entering of the time (of the ṣalāh).
10. He should make tayammum for every farḍ (ṣalāh).[47]

فصل : فُرُوضُ التَّيَمُّمِ خَمْسَةٌ :

الأَوَّلُ نَقْلُ التُّرَابِ **الثَّانِي** النِّـــيَّـــةُ **الثَّالِثُ** مَسْحُ الوَجْهِ **الرَّابِـــعُ** مَسْحُ اليَدَيْنِ إِلَى المِرْفَقَيْنِ **الْـــخَامِسُ** التَّرتِيبُ بَيْنَ المَسْحَتَيْنِ .

Section: The Integrals of Tayammum are Five:

1. Transfer of earth (to the body).[48]
2. Intention.[49]
3. Wiping of the face.[50]

---

[46] The preferred view is that tayammum will be correct if it has been performed after the entering of the time of ṣalāh even before a person determines the direction of the qiblah.

[47] Several sunnahs ṣalāh can be performed with the farḍ ṣalāh, either before or after the farḍ ṣalāh.

[48] Therefore, it will not suffice to merely pass the hands over the face or arms with the intention of tayammum when they already have dust on them.

[49] The intention of making ṣalāh permissible – it will not suffice to make the intention of removing the hadath.

4. Wiping of the two hands including the elbows.
5. Following the sequence between both wipings.[51]

فصل : مُبْطِلاتُ التَّيَمُّمِ ثَلاثَةٌ :

(1) مَا أَبْطَلَ الْوُضُوءَ (2) الرِّدَّةُ (3) وَتَوَهُّمُ الـــمَاءِ إِنْ تَيَمَّمَ لِفَقْدِهِ .

Section: The Factors That Nullify Tayammum are Three.

1. Those things which nullify the ablution.
2. Apostacy.
3. Presumption that one can now obtain water (in the case where tayammum was made due to lack of water).[52]

---

[50]It is not necessary to make the earth reach the skin under the hair of the face and arms. It is however necessary to pass the hands over that part of the beard which is visible.

[51] It is necessary to pass the hand over the face before passing them over the arms.

[52] This will apply even if one sees a mirage (thinking it to be water), or sees people who may have water, but it will not break if something prevents usage of the water for wuḍūʾ. For example, one sighted water but it is only sufficient for drinking or an enemy prevents one from acquiring it.

Note: The Sunnah Way to Perform Tayammum (Dry Ablution):

1. Begin in the name of Allah, Most Merciful, Most Compassionate (to recite Bismillah completely).
2. Wipe the upper face before the lower.
3. Wipe the right arm before the left.
4. For wiping the arms, hold the palms up, placing the left hand crosswise under the right with the left hand's fingers touching the back of the fingers of the right hand, passing the left hand up-to the right wrist. Then, curling the fingers around the side of the right wrist, one passes the left hand to the right elbow, then turns the left palm so it rests on the top of the right forearm with its thumb pointed away from one before passing it back down to the wrist, where one wipes the back of the right thumb with the inside of the left thumb. One then wipes the left arm in the same manner, followed by interlacing the fingers, rubbing the palms together, and then dusting the hands off lightly.
5. One separates the fingers when striking the earth each of the two times, and one must remove one's ring for the second, before wiping the arms.

فَصْل : الَّذِي يَطْهُرُ مِن النَّجَاسَاتِ ثَلَاثَةٌ :

(1) الْخَمْرُ إِذَا تَخَلَّلَتْ بِنَفْسِهَا (2) وَجِلْدُ الْمَيْتَةِ إِذَا دُبِغَ (3) وَمَا صَارَ حَيَوَاناً .

Section: Three Types of Impurities That Can Be Purified:

1. Wine[53] that becomes vinegar on its own.[54]

2. The hide of a dead animal that is tanned.[55]

3. Creatures that are born out of filth.[56]

فَصْل : النَّجَاسَاتُ ثَلَاثٌ :

(1) مُغَلَّظَةٌ (2) وَمُخَفَّفَةٌ (3) وَمُتَوَسِّطَةٌ .

الْــمُغَلَّظَةُ نَجَاسَةُ الْكَلْبِ وَالْخِنْزِيرِ وَفَرْعِ أَحَدِهِمَا .

وَالْمُـــخَفَّفَةُ بَوْلُ الصَّبِيِّ الَّذِي لَمْ يَطْعَمْ غَيْرَ اللَّبَنِ وَلَمْ يَبْلُغِ الْحَوْلَيْنِ .

وَالْمُتَوَسِّطَةُ سَائِرُ النَّجَاسَاتِ .

---

[53] Wine or any liquid intoxicant is impure, but solid intoxicants are pure although they are unlawful to take, eat or drink.

[54] "On its own" without anything being mixed with it. If anything was mixed with the wine before it became vinegar, then turning it to vinegar does not purify it.

[55] Tanning means removing from a hide all excess blood, fat, hair, and so forth by using an acrid substance, even if be impure. Other measures such as using salt, earth, or sunlight, are insufficient. Hides of dog or pig cannot be purified by tanning. Any hair that remains after tanning has not been purified. However, a little is excusable.

[56] Such as worms that grow in carrion.

Section: Impurities are of Three Types:

1. *Mughallaẓah* (heavy).
2. *Mukhaffafah* (light).
3. *Mutawassiṭah* (moderate).

Heavy impurity is the impurity from a dog, pig, or their offspring.

Light impurity is the urine of a baby (boy) which only feeds on milk[57] and is not yet two years of age.[58]

All other remaining impurities are **moderate impurities**.[59]

فصل :

الْمُغَلَّظَة تَطْهُرُ بِسَبْعِ غَسَلاتٍ بَعْدَ إزَالَةِ عَيْنِهَا إِحْدَاهُنَّ بِتُرَابٍ .

وَالْمُخَفَّفَة تَطْهُرُ بِرَشِّ المَاءِ عَلَيهَا مَعَ الْغَلَبَةِ وَإِزَالَةِ عَيْنِهَا .

---

[57] Whether the milk of his mother or an animal's milk, pure or impure, it will not change the ruling of it being considered a light impurity.

[58] Making "*taḥnīk*" (introducing something sweet, such as a date, into the mouth of a newborn child) or giving a child medicine will not change the ruling.

[59] Example of a moderate impurity: urine, excreta, blood, pus, vomit, wine, any liquid intoxicant, *wadī*, *madhī*, slaughtered animals that may not be eaten, unslaughtered dead animals (other than aquatic life, locusts or human beings), the milk of animals that may not be eaten (other than human), the hair of unslaughtered dead animals and the hair of animals that may not be eaten (other than human) when separated from them during their life.

وَالْمُتَوَسِّطَةُ تَنْقَسِمُ عَلَى قِسْمَيْنِ عَيْنِيَّةٌ وَحُكْمِيَّةٌ :

- الْعَيْنِيَّةُ الَّتِي لَهَا لَوْنٌ وَرِيْحٌ وَطَعْمٌ فَلا بُدَّ مِن إِزَالَةِ لَوْنِهَا وَرِيْحِهَا وَطَعْمِهَا.
- وَالْحُكْمِيَّةُ الَّتِي لا لَوْنَ وَلا رِيْحَ وَلا طَعْمَ لَهَا يَكْفِيْكَ جَرْيُ الْمَاءِ عَلَيْهَا.

Section:

- **Heavy impurity** becomes pure by removing it and then washing it seven times,[60] one of which should be with earth.[61]
- **Light impurity** will be purified by removing the actual impurity and sprinkling adequate water upon it (the amount of water sprinkled should be greater than the amount of urine).
- **Moderate impurity** is of two kinds: (1) that which has a substance and (2) that without a substance.

1. That which has a substance is that which has a colour, smell and taste. It is necessary to remove its colour, smell and taste.[62]

---

[60] Something that becomes impure by contact and that is restricted to contamination by traces of moisture from dog or pig, whether saliva, urine or anything moist from them, or any of their dry parts that have become moist. If something dry such as the animal's breath or hair touches a person, it need only be removed.

[61] Earth cannot be substituted with something else like soap or detergent etc.

[62] It is wājib to remove all of its taste, even if it be difficult, and to remove both colour and smell if not difficult. If any of the smell or

2. The one which has no substance is the one that does not have a colour, smell and taste. It is sufficient that water flows over it.[63]

فصل :

أَقَلُّ الحَيْضِ يَوْمٌ وَلَيْلَةٌ وَغَالِبُهُ سِتٌّ أَو سَبْعٌ وَأَكْثَرُهُ خَمْسَةَ عَشَرَ يَوْمًا بِلَيَالِيْهَا .

أَقَلُّ الطُّهْرِ بَيْنَ الْحَيْضَتَيْنِ خَمْسَةَ عَشَرَ يَوْمًا وَغَالِبُهُ أَرْبَعَةٌ وَعِشْرُونَ يَوْمًا أَو ثَلاثَةٌ وَعِشْرُونَ يَوْمًا وَلا حَدَّ لأَكْثَرِهِ .

أَقَلُّ النِّفَاسِ مَجَّةٌ وَغَالِبُهُ أَرْبَعُونَ يومًا وَأَكْثَرُهُ سِتُّونَ يَوْمًا .

Section:

- The minimum menstrual period is a day and a night.[64] It generally lasts for six or seven days and the maximum period is 15 days and nights.[65]

---

colour alone is difficult to remove, then the fact that one of these two remains does not affect the purity. However, if both the colour and smell remain in a spot, it is not considered pure.

[63] If the effects of sun, fire, or wind remove the traces of the impurity, the ground is still not pure until water has been poured over it.

[64] It the blood ceases to flow in less than twenty-four hours, then it is not considered haiḍ (menstruation) and the woman must make-up the ṣalāh she omitted during it. If it ceases at twenty-four hours, within fifteen days, or between the two (the blood discharged discontinuously

- The minimum interval of purity between two menstruations is 15 days. Generally it lasts for 23 or 24 days and there is no maximum limit to the number of days between two menstruations.
- The minimum postnatal bleeding is a single discharge of blood. Generally it lasts for 40 days and the maximum period is 60 days.

---

within 15 days and the duration of the blood discharged is 24 hours or more), then it is haiḍ.

[65] If it exceeds fifteen days, then she is a woman with istihāḍah (chronic vaginal discharge).

Salah

Salah

فصل : أَعْذَارُ الصَّلَاةِ اثْنَانِ :

(1) النَّوْمُ (2) والنِّسْيَانُ .

Section: The Valid Excuses for Delaying the Ṣalāh from its Prescribed Time are Two:[1]

(1) Sleep[2] and (2) forgetfulness.[3]

---

[1] A third excuse is for a person who delayed the ṣalāh to combine two ṣalāhs during a journey.

[2] A person was asleep before the time of ṣalāh commenced and remained asleep until the time ended. When any ṣalāh is due but not yet performed, and one wishes to lie down for a while and he is certain to awaken in time to carry out this duty, it will be makrūh for him to sleep or lie down. However, if he is not at all certain as to whether he will wake up in time or not, it is ḥarām.

[3] A person forgot that he did not perform the ṣalāh and only remembered after the time of ṣalāh expired. This should not be due to unmindfulness due to engrossment in playing chess etc. in which case he will be sinful.

فصل : شُرُوطُ الصَّلاةِ ثَمَانِيَةٌ :

(1) طَهَارَةُ الحَـدَثَيْنِ (2) وَالطَّهَارَةُ عَنِ النَّجَاسَةِ فِي الثَّوْبِ وَالْبَدَنِ وَالْمَكَانِ

(3) وَسَتْرُ الْعَوْرَةِ (4) وَاسْتِقْبَالُ الْقِبْلَةِ (5) وَدُخُوْلُ الْوَقْتِ (6) وَالْعِلْمُ بِفَرْضِيَّتِهَا

(7) وَأَنْ لا يَعْتَقِدَ فَرْضًا مِن فُرُوضِهَا سُنَّةً (8) وَاجْتِنَابُ الْمُبْطِلاتِ .

Section: The Conditions of the ṣalāh are Eight:[4]

1. Purity from the two ritual impurities.[5]
2. Purity of the clothing, the body,[6] and the place[7] (of performing ṣalāh).
3. Covering the ʿawrah (private parts).[8]
4. Facing the qiblah.[9]

---

[4] The author does not mention Islām and *Mumayyidh* as a condition because they are well known.

[5] Purification from minor and major ritual impurity (*hadath* and *janabah* through wuḍūʾ and ritual bath respectively as well as from haiḍ and nifas).

[6] One's ṣalāh is invalid if one is holding the end of a rope connected with something impure.

[7] One's ṣalāh is valid if performed on the pure portion of a rug which is affected with some impurities, even if the rug or bed moves when one moves. The principle is that it is not permissible for a person in ṣalāh to support or carry any impurity but it is permissible for him to be supported by it, provided he is not in direct contact with the impurity.

[8] It is a necessary condition that the clothing prevents the colour of the skin from being exposed and covers the ʿawrah from all sides including above. It is not necessary to cover the ʿawrah from below. A thin garment through which the colour of the skin is visible is not sufficient.

5. The commencement of the time of ṣalāh.[10]
6. Knowledge of it being farḍ.
7. Not to regard any of its farḍ acts as sunnah.[11]
8. To abstain from those factors that nullifies the ṣalāh.

الأَحْدَاثُ اثْنَانِ أَصْغَرُ وَأَكْبَرُ :

فَالأَصْغَرُ مَا أَوْجَبَ الْوُضُوءَ وَالأَكْبَرُ مَا أَوْجَبَ الغُسْلَ .

Ritual Impurities are of two types: (1) minor ritual impurities and (2) major ritual impurities.

(1) A minor ritual impurity is that which makes wuḍū᾽ wājib and (2) a major impurity is that which is makes bath wājib.

---

[9] This is a necessary condition for the five farḍ ṣalāh which must be performed while facing the proper direction of qiblah whether a person is a musāfir (traveller) or a muqīm (non-traveller), riding in a vehicle or not. A musāfir may perform sunnah ṣalāh without facing the direction of qiblah.

[10] A person must be certain about the commencement of the time of ṣalāh. If a person is uncertain about the commencement of the time of the ṣalāh which he has performed, that particular ṣalāh will not be correct, even if the ṣalāh was in fact carried out in its required time, unless he applies his ijtihad (discretion) to determine the time of the ṣalāh, in which case it will be correct. If he applies ijtihad and the ṣalāh was carried out before or after the time of the ṣalāh, the ṣalāh performed will be considered a qaḍā᾽ ṣalāh if he has qaḍā᾽ ṣalāh in his responsibility otherwise it will be considered a nafl ṣalāh.

[11] A person's ṣalāh is not invalidated if he thinks that all of the actions in ṣalāh are farḍ.

العَوْرَاتُ أَرْبَعٌ :

عَوْرَةُ الرَّجُلِ مُطْلَقًا وَالأَمَةِ فِي الصَّلاَةِ مَا بَيْنَ السُّرَّةِ وَالرُّكْبَةِ .

وَعَوْرَةُ الحُرَّةِ فِي الصَّلاةِ جَمِيعُ بَدَنِهَا مَا سِوَى الْوَجْهِ وَالْكَفَّيْنِ .

وَعَوْرَةُ الحُـــرَّةِ وَالأَمَةِ عِنْدَ الأَجَانِبِ جَمِيعُ الْبَدَنِ .

وَعِنْدَ مَحَارِمِهِمَا وَالنِّسَاءِ مَا بَيْنَ السُّرَّةِ وَالرُّكْبَةِ .

The ʿAwrahs (Private parts) are Four Types:

1. The ʿawrah of a man generally[12] and that of a slave-girl in ṣalāh is the area between the navel and the knees.[13]
2. The ʿawrah of a free woman in ṣalāh includes the whole body except the face and the two palms.
3. The ʿawrah of a free woman and that of a slave girl in the presence of a stranger is the entire body.
4. The ʿawrah of a free woman and a slave girl in the presence of a mahram (unmarriageable kin) or women is the area between the navel and the knees.

---

[12] Men includes young boys, even if they are not yet of the age of understanding. It generally means in all conditions; wether in ṣalāh or outside ṣalāh.

[13] The knees and the navel themselves are not part of the ʿawrah, but it is wājib to cover them in order to fulfil the command of covering the ʿawrah completely.

Note: Adhān (The Call for ṣalāh) and Iqāmah (The Call to Commence the ṣalāh)

- Adhān and Iqāmah are both sunnah for the farḍ ṣalāh, wether praying alone or in a second jamaah of ṣalāh.
- To call out the adhān is better than being the imām for the ṣalāh.
- The words of the adhān:

اللَّهُ أَكْبَرُ اللَّهُ أَكْبَرُ ، اللَّهُ أَكْبَرُ اللَّهُ أَكْبَرُ ،

أَشْهَدُ أَنْ لا إِلَه إِلاَّ اللَّهُ ، أَشْهَدُ أَنْ لا إِلَه إِلاَّ اللَّهُ ،

أَشْهَدُ أَنَّ مُحَمَّدًا رَسُولُ اللَّهِ ، أَشْهَدُ أَنَّ مُحَمَّدًا رَسُولُ اللَّهِ ،

حَيَّ عَلَى الصَّلَاة ، حَيَّ عَلَى الصَّلَاة ،

حَيَّ عَلَى الْفَلَاح ، حَيَّ عَلَى الْفَلَاح ،

اللَّهُ أَكْبَرُ اللَّهُ أَكْبَرُ ، لا إِلَه إِلاَّ اللَّهُ .

- It is sunnah to recite the two testifications in a low voice before calling it aloud:

أَشْهَدُ أَنْ لَا إِلَه إِلاَّ اللَّهُ ، أَشْهَدُ أَنْ لَا إِلَه إِلاَّ اللَّهُ ،

أَشْهَدُ أَنَّ مُحَمَّدًا رَسُول اللَّهِ ، أَشْهَدُ أَنَّ مُحَمَّدًا رَسُول اللَّهِ ،

- To add in the ṣubh ṣalāh before the final takbir (*Allahu Akbar*):

الصَّلاَةُ خَيْرٌ مِنَ النَّوْمِ ، الصَّلاَةُ خَيْرٌ مِنَ النَّوْمِ

- The words of the iqāmah:

اللَّهُ أَكْبَرُ اللَّهُ أَكْبَرُ ،

أَشْهَدُ أَنْ لاَ إِلَه إِلاَّ اللَّهُ ، أَشْهَدُ أَنَّ مُحَمَّدًا رَسُولُ اللَّهِ ،

حَيَّ عَلَى الصَّلاَة ، حَيَّ عَلَى الْفَلاحِ ،

قَدْ قَامَتِ الصَّلاَةُ ، قَدْ قَامَتِ الصَّلاَةُ ،

اللَّهُ أَكْبَرُ اللَّهُ أَكْبَرُ ، لاَ إِلَه إِلاَّ اللَّهُ .

When giving the adhān and iqāmah, it is mustaḥab (recommended):

- To be in the state of wuḍū', to stand, to face the qiblah, to turn the head (not the chest or feet) to the right when saying, "حَيَّ عَلَى الصَّلاَة" and to the left when saying, "حَيَّ عَلَى الْفَلاحِ".
- To call out the adhān calmly and slowly, pausing for an interval after each phrase of the adhān equal to the duration of the phrase (except for repetitions of "*Allahu akbar*"),

which are said in pairs and to give iqāmah rapidly without pausing.

- To repeat each phrase after the muadhdhin, even if in the state of *janābah* (major ritual impurity), during menstruation, or when reciting the Qur᾽ān.
- It is makrūh to call out the adhān in the state of hadath (minor ritual impurity), more severe to do so in a state of janabah (major ritual impurity), and even worse to give iqāmah while in either of these two states.
- After the words "حَيَّ عَلَى الصَّلاَة" and "حَيَّ عَلَى الفَلاحِ" one replies:

لاَ حَوْلَ وَلاَ قُوَّةَ إلاّ بِاللّهِ

- After the words "الصَّلاَةُ خَيْرٌ مِنَ النَّوْمِ" one replies:

صَدَقْتَ وَبَرَرْتَ

- After the words "قَدْ قَامَتِ الصَّلاَةُ" one replies:

أَقَامَهَا اللّـــهُ وَأَدَامَهَا

- To recite the following du῾ā after the adhān:

اللَّهُمَّ رَبَّ هَذِهِ الدَّعْوَةِ التَّامَّةِ وَالصَّلاَةِ الْقَائِمَةِ آتِ سَيِّدَنَا مُحَمَّدًا الْوَسِيلَةَ وَالْفَضِيلَةَ وَابْعَثْهُ مَقَامًا مَحْمُودًا الَّذِي وَعَدْتَهُ إِنَّكَ لاَ تُخْلِفُ الْمِيعَاد .

The conditions for the muadhdhin:

- (1) Islām, (2) m*umayyidh* (the age of understanding), (3) sanity and, (4) male if the adhān is for a jamāʿah of men.

فصل : أَرْكَانُ الصَّلاةِ سَبْعَةَ عَشَرَ :

الأَوَّلُ النِّـــيَّـــةُ **الثَّانِي** تَكْبِيرَةُ الإِحْرَامِ **الثَّالِثُ** الْقِيَامُ عَلَى الْقَادِرِ فِي الْفَرْضِ

الرَّابِـــعُ قِرَاءَةُ الْفَاتِحَةِ **الْــخَامِسُ** الرُّكُوعُ **السَّادِسُ** الطُّمَأْنِينَةُ فِيهِ **السَّابِعُ**

الاعْتِدَالُ **الثَّامِنُ** الطُّمَأْنِينَةُ فِيهِ **التَّاسِعُ** السُّجُودُ مَرَّتَيْنِ **الْعَاشِرُ** الطُّمَأْنِينَةُ فِيهِ **الْحَادِي**

عَشَرَ الْجُلُوسُ بَيْنَ السَّجْدَتَيْنِ **الثَّانِي** عَشَرَ الطُّمَأْنِينَةُ فِيهِ **الثَّالِثَ** عَشَرَ التَّشَهُّدُ

الأَخِيرُ **الرَّابِــعَ** عَشَرَ الْقُعُودُ فِيهِ **الْــخَامِسَ** عَشَرَ الصَّلاةُ عَلَى النَّبِيِّ ﷺ فِيهِ

السَّادِسَ عَشَرَ السَّلامُ **السَّابِعَ** عَشَرَ التَّرْتِيبُ .

Section: The Integrals of the ṣalāh are Seventeen:

1. Intention.[14]

2. *Takbīrat al-iḥrām* (The opening statement: "*Allahu Akbar*").[15]

---

[14] To make intention in the heart is wājib and mustaḥab to utter it with the tongue. The intention should be simultaneous with the *takbīrat al-iḥrām* and remains till the completion of the takbīr.

[15] *Takbīrat al-iḥrām* can only be in Arabic with the word, "*Allahu akbar*," or "*Allahul akbar*". The minimal valid audibility is that it can be heard through normal hearing. The imām calls out the *takbīr* aloud every time in ṣalāh. It is mustaḥab to raise the hands from the beginning of the *takbīrat al-iḥrām* to shoulder level, meaning that one's fingertips are even with the tip of the ears, thumbs with the earlobes, and palms with one's shoulders, fingers slightly outspread, the palms face the direction of qiblah and the hands are uncovered (i.e. not hidden beneath a shawl). After the takbīr, one places the hands below the chest and above the navel, grasping the left wrist with the right hand, and fixing

3. Standing in the farḍ ṣalāh for those who have the ability.[16]
4. Recitation of Sūrah al-Fātiḥah.[17]
5. Ruku‘ (bowing).[18]
6. Remaining motionless for a moment therein (ruku‘).
7. I‘tidāl (Straightening up after ruku‘).[19]
8. Remaining motionless for a moment therein (i‘tidāl)
9. Two sajdahs (prostrations).[20]
10. Remaining motionless for a moment therein (sajdah).
11. Sitting between the two sajdahs.[21]
12. Remaining motionless for a moment therein (sitting).

---

one's gaze on the place where one's forehead will prostrate. The complete *takbīrat al-iḥrām* must be made while standing.

[16] Standing is a rukn (integral) in all farḍ ṣalāh for one who can stand, whether by himself or assisted by another, however it is not a rukn in nafl ṣalāh. Standing requires that the spine be straight. One is not standing if one leans so forward that the backbone is no longer straight, or bends so that one is closer to ruku‘ (bowing) than to standing.

[17] Sūrah al-Fātiḥah can be recited from memory or by looking into the muṣḥaf etc. It is wājib to recite it in every rak‘ah of ṣalāh whether loudly or silently, whether an imām, a follower or alone.

[18] The best method is to raise one's hands and say, "*Allahu Akbar*" so that a person begins raising the hands as he starts the takbīr and when the hands are at shoulder level, he bows. It is mustaḥab to prolong the words of takbīr until one reaches the next posture in every takbīr so that no part of the ṣalāh is without dhikr. Thereafter, the hands are placed on the knees, fingers apart, with back and neck extended, leg straight and elbows out, although women keep them close, then one recites tasbih three times.

[19] The i‘tidāl is to return to the posture one was in before the ruku‘, whether one was standing or sitting. It is wājib to intend nothing by one's movement except i‘tidāl.

[20] In every rak‘ah.

[21] In every rak‘ah and to intend nothing but sitting by one's movement.

13. Recite tashahhud at the end of ṣalāh.
14. Sitting therein (tashahhud).
15. Ṣalāh upon Nabi ﷺ therein (tashahhud).
16. Salām.[22]
17. To follow the sequence (of the above integral postures of ṣalāh).

[22] Ending the ṣalāh with salām. Someone who is not a masbūq (latecomer) to a jamāʿah ṣalāh may sit as long as he wishes after the imām's salām to supplicate, finishing with his own salām whenever he wishes.

Note: Description of the Ṣalāh:

Sunan Before Commencing the Ṣalāh:

To stand for the ṣalāh after the completion of the iqāmah, to be in the first row, to make the row straight, especially for the imām when he should enjoin upon the jamāʿah to do so and to fill up the first row first, then the second, and so on.

Commencing the Ṣalāh:

One starts to make the ***takbīrat al-iḥrām*** with the intention in the heart. It is mustaḥab to recite the duʿā iftitah after the *takbīrat al-iḥrām*.

After the ***duʿā iftitaḥ***, it is mustaḥab to recite the *taʿawwudh*. ***Taʿawwudh*** is mustaḥab in every rakʿah and more emphasized in the first rakʿah. Then a person recites **Sūrah al-Fātiḥah** in every rakʿah and the basmalah is one of its verses. One says "***Āmīn***" at the end of the al-Fātiḥah, when following an imām, one says "Āmīn" when he does, and then a second time when he completes his own recital of the al-Fātiḥah.

If one is the imām or praying alone, it is mustaḥab in the first and second rakʿah only to recite one complete **sūrah** even if it be short after the al-Fātiḥah. It is mustaḥab to recite the Qurʾān in a tartīl (distinct and pleasant way) observing the rules of tajwīd and to reflect upon its meanings and lessons. One recites a longer sūrah in the first rakʿah than in the second.

Then one makes **rukuʿ** (bows) from the waist. The best way is to raise one's hands and say, "*Allahu akbar*" so that a person begins raising the hands as he starts the takbir and when the hands are at shoulder level, he bows. It is mustaḥab to prolong the words of takbir until one reaches the posture of rukuʿ.

Then one makes ***iʿtidāl*** (straightening up), the best way is to raise the hand lifting them from the knees as one starts straightening up, raising them to shoulder level and the head together, saying, "*samiʿallahu liman ḥamidah.*" When one is standing upright, one says, "*Rabbanā lakal ḥamd.*"

Then one makes **sajdah** (prostrates), the best way is to say, "*Allahu Akbar,*" and to put the knees down first, then the hands, and then the forehead and nose, keeping the hands directly under one's shoulders, with the fingers together, extended towards the direction of qiblah, and the hands uncovered. For men to maintain a one span gap between the two knees and two feet whilst women keep them together. For men to keep the stomach away from the thighs, and forearms from the sides, whilst women keep them together, and to recite "*tasbīh*" three times. It is commendable to supplicate before Allah ﷻ while prostrating.

Then one **raises the head and sits before prostrating a second time**, the best way is to say, "*Allahu akbar,*" as one raises the head, to sit in "*iftirāsh*," which is to place the left foot on its side and to sit upon it while keeping the right foot on the bottom of its toes, heel up. To place both one's hands on the thighs near the knees, fingers extended and held together and to recite the duʿā, "*Rabbighfirlī, warḥamnī, wajburnī, warfaʿnī, warzuqnī, wahdinī, waʿāfinī, waʿfuʿannī.*"

Then one **prostrates again just as before** and after this one raises the head, saying, "*Allahu akbar,*" as one first raises it, prolonging the takbir until one is standing upright.

It is sunnah, here and in each rakʿah that is not followed by the tashahhud, to briefly rest in the ***iftirāsh*** style of sitting before rising. Then one rises, supported by both hands, palms down, and prolonging the takbir until standing. This is called "***jilsat al-istirāhah***" and is not done after "*sajdah al-tilawah*".

Then one performs the second rakʿah of the ṣalāh just like the first, except for the initial intention, the *takbīrat al-iḥrām*, and duʿā iftitah.

If one's **ṣalāh exceeds two rakʿahs**, one sits in iftirāsh after the first two rakʿahs and recites the tashahhud and the ṣalāh upon the Nabi ﷺ, but not upon his family (which is done in the final tashahhud). Then one rises, saying, "*Allahu akbar,*" and supported on one's hands as before. When standing, one raises the hands to shoulder level (which one does here, but not after rising form the first or third rakʿah), and then goes on to perform the remainder of the ṣalāh as one did in the second rakʿah, except that one recites the al-Fātiḥah to oneself and does not recite a sūrah after it.

One sits at the end of one's ṣalāh for the **last tashahhud** in the "***tawarruk***" style of sitting, with one left posterior on the ground and left foot on its side, emerging from under the right, which is vertical.

In the two tashahhuds, the left hand rests on the left thigh near the knee, its fingers extended and held together. The right hand is similarly placed, but is held closed with its thumb touching the side of the index finger, which alone is left extended. One raises the index finger and points with it when one says the words, "*illallah,*" in the tashahhud.

Closing the ṣalāh:

Then one says the final "***salām***". The best way is to say, "*Assalāmu ʿalaykum waraḥmatullah,*" and to turn the head to the right enough to show the right cheek to those behind. One thereby intends to finish the ṣalāh and intends to make salām to the Angels and Muslims whether human or jinn on the right. Then turns one's head to the left and repeat the salām, intending to greet those on the left. The follower may intend one of the salāms to be a response to the salām of the imām.

It is mustaḥab **to make dhikr and duʿā silently after ṣalāh**. Al-Imām al-Shāfiʿī mentioned in al-Umm, "I prefer that the imām and follower make dhikr after the salām, and do so silently, unless the imām wants to be learned from, in which case he says the dhikr aloud until he believes that the congregation has learned from him, after which he will say it silently."

The imām turns for dhikr and duʿā so that his right side is towards the jamāʿah and his left side towards the qiblah. He leaves his place as soon as he finishes. If there are no women (in which case he waits for them to leave first). It is mustaḥab for the followers to remain seated until the imām stands.

فصل : النِّيَّةُ ثلاَثُ دَرَجَاتٍ :

إِنْ كَانَتِ الصَّلاَةُ فَرْضاً وَجَبَ قَصْدُ الْفِعْلِ وَالتَّعْيِينُ وَالفَرْضِيّةُ .

وَإِن كَانَتْ نَافِلَةً مُؤَقَّتَةً كَرَاتِبَةٍ أَوْ ذَاتِ سَبَبٍ وَجَبَ قَصْدُ الْفِعْلِ وَالتَّعْيِينُ.

وَإِنْ كَانَتْ نَافِلَةً مُطْلَقَةً وَجَبَ قَصْدُ الْفِعْلِ فَقَطْ .

الْفِعْلُ أُصَلِّي وَالتَّعْيِينُ ظُهْرًا أَوْ عَصْرًا وَالْفَرْضِيَّةُ فَرْضًا .

Section: There are Three Degrees of Intention:

If the ṣalāh is farḍ, it is compulsory to intend:[23]

a. The act of ṣalāh – the intention of performing ṣalāh.
b. The actual ṣalāh that is being offered e.g. Ẓuhr or ʿAṣr.
c. It being a farḍ ṣalāh.

If the ṣalāh is a periodic nafl like "*rawātīb*"[24] or it has a specific reason[25], it is compulsory to intend:

a. The act of ṣalāh – the intention of performing ṣalāh.
b. The actual ṣalāh that is being offered e.g. sunnah before ṣubh or "*Istisqā'*" (ṣalāh seeking rain).

If the ṣalāh is a muṭlaq nafl,[26] it is compulsory to intend:

a. The act of ṣalāh – the intention of performing ṣalāh.

---

[23] It is sufficient for a person to make intention to offer the farḍ ṣalāh of Ẓuhr.

[24] Those sunnah ṣalāh performed either before or after the five farḍ ṣalāh.

[25] Like the ṣalāh of ʿEid al-Fiṭr or ṣalāh al-istisqāʾ (seeking rain). It is sufficient that a person makes intention to offer ṣalāh of 'Eid al-Fiṭr or al-istisqāʾ.

[26] Those nafl ṣalāh that have no time or cause. A person performs them when one wants for additional rewards. It is sufficient to merely make the intention of performing ṣalāh for these ṣalāh.

فصل : شُرُوطُ تَكْبِيرَةِ الإِحْرَامِ سِتَّةَ عَشَرَ :

(1) أَنْ تَقَعَ حَالَةَ الْقِيَامِ فِي الفَرْضِ (2) وَأَنْ تَكُونَ بِالْعَرَبِيَّةِ (3) وَأَنْ تَكُونَ بِلَفْظِ

الْجَلَالَةِ (4) وَبِلَفْظِ أَكْبَرُ (5) والتَّرتِيبُ بَيْنَ اللَّفْظَيْنِ (6) وَأَنْ لَا يَمُدَّ هَمْزَةَ

الْجَلَالَةِ (7) وَعَدَمُ مَدِّ بَاءِ أَكْبَرُ (8) وَأَنْ لَا يُشَدِّدَ الْبَاءَ (9) وأَنْ لَا يَزِيدَ وَاوًا

سَاكِنَةً أَوْ مُتَحَرِّكَةً بَيْنَ الكَلِمَتَيْنِ (10) وَأَنْ لَا يَزِيدَ وَاوًا قَبْلَ الْجَلَالَةِ (11) وَأَنْ

لَا يَقِفَ بَيْنَ كَلِمَتَي التَّكْبِيرِ وَقْفَةً طَوِيلَةً وَلَا قَصِيرَةً (12) وَأَنْ يُسْمِعَ نَفْسَهُ جَمِيعَ

حُرُوفِهَا (13) وَدُخُولُ الْوَقْتِ فِي الْمُؤَقَّتِ (14) وَإِيقَاعُهَا حَالَ الاسْتِقْبَالِ (15)

وَأَنْ لَا يُخِلَّ بِحَرْفٍ مِن حُرُوفِهَا (16) وَتَأْخِيرُ تَكْبِيرَةِ الْمَأْمُومِ عَنْ تَكْبِيرَةِ الْإِمَامِ .

Section: The Conditions of *Takbīrat al-iḥrām* are Sixteen:

1. That it is pronounced while standing in the farḍ ṣalāh.

2. That it be in Arabic.

3. That it be with the word "*Allahu*".

4. That it be with the word "*akbar*".

5. The sequence between these two words "*Allahu akbar*" is followed.

6. Not to lengthen the *hamzah* of the word "*Allah*".[27]

---

[27] By reciting it as "*Āllahu akbar*," this can result in the meaning changing.

7. Not to lengthen the letter of "*ba*" of "*akbar*".[28]
8. Not to double the letter of "*ba*".[29]
9. Not to add a "*waw*" *sakin* or *mutaharrik* between these two words.[30]
10. Not to add a "waw" before the word "Allah".
11. Not to pause for a long or short while between these two words.
12. To hear oneself uttering its entire letters.[31]
13. Entering of the time of ṣalāh.
14. For it to occur while facing towards the qiblah.
15. Not to change even a single letter.
16. To delay the takbir of the maʾmūm (follower) till after the takbir of the imām.

فصل : شُرُوطُ الْفَاتِحَةِ عَشَرَةٌ :

(1) التَّرتِيبُ (2) والْمُوَالاَةُ (3) وَمُرَاعَاةُ حُرُوفِهَا (4) وَمُراعَاةُ تَشْدِيدَاتِهَا (5)

وَأَنْ لاَ يَسْكُتَ سَكْتَةً طَوِيلَةً وَلا قَصيرَةً يَقْصِدُ بِهَا قَطْعَ الْقِرَاءَةِ (6) وَقِرَاءَةُ كُلِّ

[28] By reciting it as "*Allahu akbār*," this can result in the meaning changing.
[29] By reciting it with the *tashdīd.*
[30] By reciting it as "*Allahū akbar*" or "*Allahu wakbar*".
[31] That one can hear them oneself, given normal hearing and lack of extraneous noise. There is no need to raise one's voice if there is lot of noise.

آياتِهَا وَمِنهَا البَسْمَلَةُ (7) وَعَدَمُ اللَّحْنِ الـــمُخِلِّ بِالمَعْنَى (8) وَأَنْ تَكُونَ حَالَةَ الْقِيَامِ فِي الْفَرْضِ (9) وَأن يُسْمِعَ نَفْسَهُ القِرَاءَةَ (10) وَأَنْ لا يَتَخَلَّلَهَا ذِكْرٌ أَجْنَبِيٌّ.

Section: The Conditions of Sūrah al-Fātiḥah are Ten:

1. Sequence.
2. Continuity.[32]
3. To perfect (pronunciation of) it's letters.
4. To perfect it's tashdīds.
5. Not to pause for a long or short while with the intention of terminating the recitation.
6. Reciting all its verses including the "*basmalah*".
7. Not to commit a mistake that alters the meaning.[33]
8. To recite it while standing in the farḍ ṣalāh.[34]
9. To hear one's own recitation.

---

[32] The al-Fātiḥah is not considered to be interrupted if a one replies to the "*Āmīn*" of the imām, reminding him of the right ayat (verse) when he errs, prostrates with the imām in "*sajdah tilāwah*", forgetfully falls silent or absentmindedly adds some dhikr in it.

[33] If one omits one of the al-Fātiḥah's letters, fails to double a letter that should be doubled, or substitutes a wrong letter for the right one, it invalidates one's recital of that particular word, and one must recite that word again. This will not invalidate one's ṣalāh unless it changes the meaning and was done deliberately. Mistakes in a harakah (short vowel) are not harmful as long as they do not alter the meaning.

[34] Its entire letters should be recited while standing.

10. No foreign dhikr or recitation should be recited in-between (the al-Fātiḥah).

فصل : تَشْدِيدَاتُ الفَاتِحَةِ أَرْبَعَ عَشْرَةً :

بِسْمِ اللّـٰـهِ فَوْق اللامِ الرَّحْمن فَوْقَ الرَّاءِ الرَّحِيمِ فَوْقَ الرَّاءِ . الْحَمْدُ لِلّهِ فَوْقَ لامِ الْجَلالَةِ رَبِّ الْعَالَمِينَ فَوْقَ البَاءِ . الرَّحْمنِ فَوْق الرَّاءِ الرَّحِيمِ فَوْق الرَّاءِ. مَالِكِ يَوْمِ الدِّين فَوْقَ الدَّالِ . إِيَّاكَ نَعْبُدُ فَوْقَ اليَاءِ وَإِيَّاكَ نَسْتَعِينُ فَوْقَ اليَاءِ. إِهْدِنَا الصِّرَاطَ الْمُسْتَقِيمَ فَوْقَ الصَّادِ . صِرَاطَ الَّذِيْنَ فَوْقَ اللامِ أَنْعَمْتَ عَلَيْهِمْ غَيْرِ المَغْضُوبِ عَلَيْهِمْ وَلا الضَّالِّينَ فَوْقَ الضَّادِ وَاللامِ.

Section: There are 14 tashdīds that are recited on various word of Sūrah al-Fātiḥah which are demonstrated in the following diagram:

بسم اللّٰـه الرّحمن الرّحيم . الحمد لـلّٰـه ربّ العالمين . الرّحمن الرّحيم. مالك يوم الدّين . إيّـاك نعبد وإيّـاك نستعين . إهدنا الصّراط المستقيم. صراط الّذين أنعمت عليهم غير المغضوب عليهم ولا الضّالّـين .

فصل : يُسَنُّ رَفْعُ الْيَدَيْنِ فِي أَرْبَعَةِ مَوَاضِعَ :

(1) عِنْدَ تَكْبِيرَةِ الإِحْرَامِ (2) وَعِنْدَ الرُّكُوعِ (3) وَعِنْدَ الاعْتِدَالِ (4) وَعِنْدَ الْقِيَامِ مِنَ التَّشَهُّدِ الأَوَّلِ .

Section: It is Sunnah to Raise the Hands in Four Places:[35]

1. During the *takbīrat al-iḥrām*.[36]
2. When going into *rukū'*.[37]
3. When straightening up (*i'itidāl*).[38]
4. When standing up from the first *tashahhud.*

فصل : شُرُوطُ السُّجُودِ سَبْعَةٌ :

(1) أَنْ يَسْجُدَ عَلَى سَبْعَةِ أَعْضَاءٍ (2) وَأَنْ تَكُونَ جَبْهَتُهُ مَكْشُوفَةً (3) وَالتَّحَامُلُ بِرَأْسِهِ (4) وَعَدَمُ الْهُوِيِّ لِغَيْرِهِ (6) وَأَنْ لا يَسْجُدَ عَلَى شَيْءٍ يَتَحَرَّكُ بِحَرَكَتِهِ (7) وَارْتِفَاعُ أَسَافِلِهِ عَلَى أَعَالِيهِ (8) والطُّمَأْنِينَةُ فِيهِ .

---

[35] It is from the "*sunan hay'ah*" of the ṣalāh, the wisdom being to show respect and reverence to Allah ﷻ.

[36] Begin raising the hands at the beginning of the takbīr and put them down at the end of the takbīr, means that raising of the hands must be simultaneous with the takbīr from the beginning till the end.

[37] A person starts raising his hands at the beginning of takbīr and prolongs the takbīr until he places his hands upon his knees, fingers spread apart and backbone and head are straight.

[38] A person begins raising his hand with the raising of the head and the takbīr; when he straightens, he lowers his hands.

خَاتِمَةٌ أَعضَاءُ السُّجُودِ سَبْعَةٌ :

الْجَبْهَةُ وَبُطُونِ الْكَفَّيْنِ وَالرُّكْبَتَانِ وَبُطُونُ أصَابع الرِّجْلَيْن .

Section: The Conditions of Sajdah (Prostration) are Seven:

1. To prostrate upon seven limbs.[39]
2. The forehead should be exposed.[40]
3. To make sajdah by resting on the head.[41]
4. Not to intend anything but sajdah.[42]
5. Not to prostrate on something that moves with one's own movement.
6. That one rear's be higher than one's head.
7. Remain motionless for a moment whilst prostrating.

The Seven Limbs of Prostration are:

The forehead, both palms, both knees and the portion under the toes of each foot.

---

[39] It is sunnah to place the nose on the ground, however, sajdah will be in order if the nose does not touch the ground.

[40] If one is wearing a bandage over the forehead because of an injury, sajdah may be made on the bandage without the need of repeating it afterwards with the condition that the bandage was put on while one was in the state of purity.

[41] The weight of the head and neck should be applied to the place of sajdah so that the forehead is firmly stationed on the ground.

[42] If one merely fell down after the iʿtidāl, this will not be regarded as sajdah. The person will have to return to iʿtidāl and then go into sajdah.

فصل : تَشْدِيدَاتُ التَّشَهُّدِ إِحْدَى وَعِشْرُونَ :

خَمْسٌ فِي أَكْمَلِهِ وَسِتَّةَ عَشَرَ فِي أَقَلِّهِ .

التَّحِيَّاتُ عَلَى التَّاءِ وَالْيَاءِ الْمُبَارَكَاتُ الصَّلَوَاتُ عَلَى الصَّادِ الطَّيِّبَاتُ عَلَى الطَّاءِ وَالْيَاءِ لِلَّـــهِ عَلَى لامِ الْجَلالَةِ. السَّلامُ عَلَى السِّين عَلَيْكَ أَيُّهَا النَّبِيُّ عَلَى الْيَاءِ وَالنُونِ وَالْيَاءِ وَرَحْمَةُ اللَّـــهِ عَلَى لامِ الْجَلالَةِ وَبَرَكَاتُهُ . السَّلامُ عَلَى السِّين عَلَيْنَا وَعَلَى عِبَادِ اللَّـــهِ عَلَى لامِ الْجَلالَةِ الصَّالِحِينَ عَلَى الصَّادِ. أَشْهَدُ أَنْ لا إِلهَ عَلَى لامِ أَلِفٍ إِلا اللَّـــهُ عَلَى لامِ أَلِفٍ وَلامِ الْجَلالَةِ. وَأَشْهَدُ أَنَّ عَلَى النُّونِ مُحَمَّدًا رَسُولُ اللَّـــهِ عَلَى مِيمِ مُحَمَّدٍ وَعَلَى الرَّاءِ وَعَلَى لامِ الْجَلالَةِ.

Section: There are 21 tashdīds that are recited in tashahhud, five are their completion and 16 are minimal of the tashahhud[43], all are demonstrated in the following diagram:

[43] The minimal tashahhud is:

التحيّات للّـــه . سلام عليك أيّها النبّـــيّ ورحمة اللّـــه وبركاته . سلام علينا وعلى عباد اللّـــه الصالحين . أشهد أن لاّ إله إلاّ اللّـــه وأشهد أنّ محمّدا رّسول اللّـــه

التحيّات المباركات الصلوات الطيّبات للّـه . السلام عليك أيّها النبيّ ورحمة

اللّـه وبركاته . السلام علينا وعلى عباد اللّـه الصالحين . أشهد أن لاّ إله إلاّ

اللّـه وأشهد أنّ محمّدا رّسول اللّـه .

فصل : تَشْدِيدَاتُ أَقَلِّ الصَّلاةِ عَلَى النَّبِيِّ أَرْبَعٌ :

اللَّهُمَّ عَلَى اللامِ وَالْمِيمِ صَلِّ عَلَى اللامِ عَلَى مُحَمَّدٍ عَلَى الْمِيمِ .

Section: There are 4 tashdīds for the minimal ṣalāh upon Nabi ﷺ:

اللّهمّ صلّ على محمّد .

فصل : أَقَلُّ السَّلامِ السَّلامُ عَلَيْكُمْ .

تَشْدِيدُ السَّلام عَلَى السِّينِ .

Section: The minimal salām is "*Assalāmu ʿalaykum*":

There is one tashdīd in salām: السّلام عليكم

فَصْل : أَوْقَاتُ الصَّلَاةِ خَمْسٌ :

أَوَّلُ وَقْتِ **الظُّهْر** زَوَالُ الشَّمْسِ وَآخِرُهُ مَصِيرُ ظِلِّ الشَّيْءِ مِثْلَهُ غَيْرَ ظِلِّ الاسْتِوَاءِ .

وَأَوَّلُ وَقْتِ **الْعَصْرِ** إِذَا صَارَ ظِلُّ كُلِّ شَيْءٍ مِثْلَهُ وَزَادَ قَلِيلًا وَآخِرُهُ غُرُوبُ الشَّمْسِ

. وَأَوَّلُ وَقْتِ **الْمَغْرِب** غُرُوبُ الشَّمْسِ وَآخِرُهُ غُرُوبُ الشَّفَقَ الْأَحْمَرِ . وَأَوَّلُ

وَقْتِ **الْعِشَاء** غُرُوبُ الشَّفَقِ الْأَحْمَرِ وَآخِرُهُ طُلُوعُ الْفَجْرِ الصَّادِقِ. وَأَوَّلُ وَقْتِ

الصُّبْح طُلُوعُ الْفَجْرِ الصَّادِقِ وَآخِرُهُ طُلُوعُ الشَّمْسِ .

الْأَشْفَاقُ ثَلَاثَةٌ أَحْمَرُ وَأَصْفَرُ وَأَبْيَضُ .

الْأَحْمَرُ مَغْرِبٌ وَالْأَصْفَرُ وَالْأَبْيَضُ عِشَاءٌ وَيُنْدَبُ تَأْخِيرُ صَلَاةِ الْعِشَاءِ إِلَى أَنْ يَغِيبَ

الشَّفَقُ الْأَصْفَرُ وَالْأَبْيَضُ .

Section: The Times of ṣalāh are Five:[44]

- The time of Ẓuhr begins after the sun descends from its zenith (*zawāl*) and it ends when an object's shadow equals its length in addition to the length of its shadow at the time of *zawāl*.
- The time of ʿAṣr begins when the object's shadow equals its length in addition to the length of its shadow at the time of *zawāl*, and ends when the sun sets.
- The time of Maghrīb begins from sunset and ends with the disappearance of the red horizon.
- The time of ʿIshāʾ begins from the setting of the red horizon and it ends at ṣubh sadiq.
- The time of Ṣubh begins from the dawn until sunrise.

There are three types of horizons; red, yellow and white:

- The red horizon is at the time of Maghrīb, while the yellow and white are at the time of ʿIshāʾ. It is sunnah to delay the ṣalāh of ʿIshāʾ till the yellow and white horizons disappear.

[44] It is best to pray every prayer at the beginning of its time, taking the necessary steps at its outset, such as purification, clothing one's ʿawrah, giving the adhan and iqamah, and then praying. If less than one rakʿah of one's ṣalāh occurs within the proper time (meaning that one does not raise one's head from the second sajdah of the rakʿah before the time ends) and the remainder takes place after it, then the entire ṣalāh is considered as qaḍāʾ. It is not permissible to intentionally delay the ṣalāh until part of it is prayed after the time has terminated.

فصل : تَحْرُمُ الصَّلَاةُ الَّتِي لَيْسَ لَهَا سَبَبٌ مُتَقَدِّمٌ وَلَا مُقَارِنٌ فِي خَمْسَةِ أَوْقَاتٍ :

(1) عِنْدَ طُلُوعِ الشَّمْسِ حَتَّى تَرْتَفِعَ قَدْرَ رُمْحٍ (2) وَعِنْدَ الاسْتِوَاءِ فِي غَيْرِ يَوْمِ الْجُمُعَةِ حَتَّى تَزُولَ (3) وَعِنْدَ الاصْفِرَارِ حَتَّى تَغْرُبَ (4) وَبَعْدَ صَلَاةِ الصُّبْحِ حَتَّى تَطْلُعَ الشَّمْسُ (5) وَبَعْدَ صَلَاةِ الْعَصْرِ حَتَّى تَغْرُبَ .

Section: There are 5 times in a day during which it is ḥarām[45] to offer those ṣalāhs which do not have an immediate or preceding cause:[46]

1. At the time of sunrise until the sun rises to the extent of the height of a spear.
2. At the time when the sun is at its zenith until it declines, except on Fridays.
3. At the time the sun becomes yellow/pale until sunset.
4. After Ṣubh ṣalāh until sunrise.
5. After ʿAṣr ṣalāh until sunset.

---

[45] It is neither ḥarām nor makrūh to offer ṣalāh within the Sanctuary of Makkah at any time.

[46] The ṣalāh is unlawful and invalid and it will not discharge a person from a vow. It is permissible at the above times to offer ṣalāh that are performed for a particular reason, such as the *salat al-janazah* (funeral ṣalāh), *taḥiyyat al-masjīd* (greeting the mosque), sunnah after wuḍūʾ, and is also permissible to make *qaḍāʾ* ṣalāh though one may not perform the two rakʿahs that are sunnah before entering the state of iḥrām.

فصل : سَكَتَاتُ الصَّلاةِ سِتَّةٌ :

(1) بَيْنَ تَكْبِيرَةِ الإِحْرَامِ وَدُعَاءِ الافْتِتَاحِ (2) وَبَيْنَ دُعَاءِ الافْتِتَاحِ وَالتَّعَوُّذِ (3)

وَبَيْنَ الفَاتِحَةِ وَالتَّعَوُّذِ (4) وَبَيْنَ آخِرِ الفَاتِحَةِ وَآمِين (5) وَبَيْنَ آمِين وَالسُّورَةِ (6)

وَبَيْنَ السُّورَةِ وَالرُّكُوعِ .

Section: The Pauses in ṣalāh are Six:[47]

1. Between the *takbīrat al-iḥrām* and the "*du'ā iftitah*" (the opening du'ā).[48]
2. Between the "*du'ā iftitah*" (the opening du'ā) and *ta'awwudh*[49].
3. Between the *ta'awwudh* and Sūrah al-Fātiḥah.
4. Between the completion of Sūrah al-Fātiḥah and saying, "*Āmīn*".
5. Between "*Āmīn*" and the sūrah.
6. Between the sūrah and bowing (ruku').

[47] It is mustaḥab to pause for the duration of one tasbih (duration of reciting one "*subḥānallah*").

[48] It is mustaḥab for the imām to remain silent for the time that a follower can recite Sūrah al-Fātiḥah and for him to engage in the recitation of the Qur'ān or du'ā silently.

[49] Ta'awwudh is to recite "*A'ūdhubillahi minash shaiṭānir rajīm*".

فصل : الأَرْكَانُ الَّتِي تَلْزَمُهُ فِيهَا الطُّمَأنِينَةُ أَرْبَعَةٌ :

(1) الرُّكُوعُ (2) والاعْتِدَالُ (3) وَالسُّجُودُ (4) وَالْجُلُوسُ بَيْنَ السَّجْدَتَيْنِ .

الطُّمَأنِينَةُ هِيَ سُكُونٌ بَعْدَ حَرَكَةٍ بِحَيْثُ يَسْتَقِرُّ كُلُّ عُضْوٍ مَحَلَّهُ بِقَدْرِ سُبْحَانَ اللّـــهِ .

Section: There are Four Postures in Which Ṭumaʾnīnah (Composure) is Compulsory:

1. In ruku‘.
2. In i‘tidāl (when straightening up after ruku‘).
3. In sajdah.
4. While sitting between the two sajdahs.

Ṭumaʾnīnah (composure) is a pause after movements to such an extent that every limb remains in its place for the duration of reciting one “*subḥānallah*”.

فصل : أَسبَابُ سُجُودِ السَّهْوِ أَرْبَعَةٌ :

الأَوَّلُ تَرْكُ بَعْضٍ مِنْ أَبْعَاضِ الصَّلاةِ أَوْ بَعْضِ الْبَعْضِ **الثَّاني** فِعْلُ مَا يُبْطِلُ عَمْدُهُ وَلا يُبْطِلُ سَهْوُهُ إِذَا فَعَلَهُ نَاسِياً **الثَّالِثُ** نَقْلُ رُكْنٍ قَوْلِيٍّ إِلَى غَيْرِ مَحَلِّهِ **الرَّابِـــعُ** إِيقَاعُ رُكْنٍ فِعْلِيٍّ مَعَ احْتِمَالِ الزِّيَادَةِ .

Section: The Causes for Sajdah Sahw[50] (Prostration of Forgetfulness) are Four:

1. Leaving out some of the "*sunan abʿaḍ*" (main sunnah), either completely or partly.[51]
2. To forgetfully do an action that would nullify the ṣalāh if it was done intentionally.[52]
3. To recite a verbal integral of ṣalāh in an inappropriate place.[53]
4. To perform a physical integral with the possibility of it being an extra integral.[54]

---

[50] The sajdah sahw, even if there are numerous reasons for it in one ṣalāh, is only two sajdahs (prostrations).

[51] If one misses a *sunnat abʿaḍ* (main sunnah) even purposely, one performs sajdah sahw. If one misses anything besides a rukn (integral) or sunnat abʿaḍ (main sunnah), then one does not postrate for it. If one forgets the first tashahhud and stands up, it is not permissible to retun to it. If one intentionally returns to it, this invalidates one's ṣalāh, but if one returns to it absentmindedly or out of ignorance, one merely prostrates for it, though one must stand up as soon as one remembers.

[52] Such as turning the head, taking one or two steps, lengthening a short integral like iʿtidāl or a little speech, provided it is not the type of action whose unintentional performance also invalidates the ṣalāh such as much speech or action, since doing it would in any case invalidate the ṣalāh.

[53] Such as reciting a part or all of the al-Fātiḥah or tashahhud at the wrong place. This will not apply to the *tasbīḥāt* even though one did so purposely.

[54] When one is uncertain whether he or she has prayed three rakʿahs or four, one should assume that he or she did not perform it.

فصل : أَبْعَاضُ الصَّلاةِ سَبْعَةٌ :

(1) التَّشَهُّدُ الأَوَّلُ (2) وَقُعُودُهُ (3) وَالصَّلاةُ عَلَى النَّبِيِّ ﷺ فِيهِ (4) وَالصَّلاةُ عَلَى الآلِ فِي التَّشَهُّدِ الأَخِيرِ (5) وَالْقُنُوتُ (6) وَالصَّلاةُ وَالسَّلامُ عَلَى النَّبِيِّ ﷺ (7) وآلِهِ وَصَحْبِهِ فِيهِ .

Section: The Sunan Abʿaḍ[55] (Main Sunnahs) of ṣalāh are Seven:

1. The recitation of the first tashahhud.[56]
2. The sitting therein (in the first tashahhud).
3. The recitation of *ṣalāh* upon Nabi ﷺ therein (in the first tashahhud).[57]
4. The recitation of *ṣalāh* upon his family in the final tashahhud.
5. The recitation of duʿā Qunūt.
6. The recitation of *ṣalāh* and *salām* upon Nabi ﷺ (in duʿā Qunūt).
7. The recitation of *ṣalāh* and *salām* upon his family and his Companions therein (in duʿā Qunūt).

---

[55] Sunan abʿaḍ are those sunnah acts that if omitted can be compensated for by sajdah sahw. On the other hand, those sunnah acts that cannot be compensated for by sajdah sahw are called sunan hay'ah.

[56] If the imām left out the first tashahhud, it is not permissible for the follower to act contrary to the imām i.e. the follower will have to also follow the imām in this act.

[57] If the imām lengthens the first tashahhud for a valid reason and the follower completed the first tashahhud before the imām, the follower should not continue and recite the ṣalāh upon the family of Nabī ﷺ, rather he should occupy himself with duʿā.

فصل : تَبْطُلُ الصَّلاةُ بِأَرْبَعَ عَشْرَةَ خَصْلَةً :

(1) بِالْحَدَثِ (2) وَبِوُقُوعِ النَّجَاسَةِ إِنْ لَمْ تُلْقَ حَالا مِنْ غَيْرِ حَمْلٍ (3) وَانْكِشَافِ الْعَوْرَةِ إِنْ لَمْ تُسْتَرْ حَالا (4) وَالنُّطْقِ بِحَرْفَيْنِ أَوْ حَرْفٍ مُفْهِمٍ عَمْدًا (5) وَبِالْمُفْطِرِ عَمْدًا (6) وَالأَكْلِ الْكَثِيرِ نَاسِيا (7) وَثَلاثِ حَرَكَاتٍ مُتَوَالِيَاتٍ وَلَوْ سَهْوًا (8) وَالْوَثْبَةِ الْفَاحِشَةِ (9) وَالضَّرْبَةِ الْمُفْرِطَةِ (10) وَزِيَادَةِ رُكْنٍ فِعْلِيٍّ عَمْدًا (11) وَالتَّقَدُّمِ عَلَى إِمَامِهِ بِرُكْنَيْنِ فِعْلِيَّيْنِ (12) وَالتَّخَلُّفِ بِهِمَا بِغَيْرِ عُذْرٍ (13) وَنِيَّةِ قَطْعِ الصَّلاةِ وَتَعْلِيقِ قَطْعِهَا بِشَيْءٍ (14) وَالتَّرَدُّدِ فِي قَطْعِهَا .

Section: The Factors Which Nullify the ṣalāh are Fourteen:

1. Hadath (ritual impurity).[58]
2. Impurity falling on the body or clothes[59] if not removed immediately[60]without carrying it.[61]
3. Exposing of the ʿawrah if it was not covered immediately.[62]

---

[58] Even unintentionally, if a person forgot to perform wuḍūʾ and offers a ṣalāh, this ṣalāh will not be valid.

[59] If an imām led a jamāʿah while there was impurity on his clothes, the entire jamāʿah will have to repeat the ṣalāh if the impurity was visible to others or if it was in such a place that all could have seen it. If it was not visible, the imām alone will have to repeat the ṣalāh.

[60] Not more than the minimum amount of one tasbih.

[61] By removing the impurity – for example with the side of a stone or a stick without carrying the stone or stick.

4. Intentionally uttering one or two letters which can be clearly understood.[63]
5. To break the fast intentionally (in ṣalāh).[64]
6. To forgetfully eat a lot.[65]
7. Three consecutive motions even if involuntarily.[66]
8. Extra movement that is contrary to the habit of a sane person.[67]
9. An excessive strike of the hand.[68]

---

[62] When the ʿawrah of a person becomes exposed even slightly, the ṣalāh is invalidated. However, if it was exposed because of wind and it is covered up immediately with little movement, the ṣalāh remain valid. If much movement is done to cover the exposed part, the ṣalāh will be invalidated.

[63] The ṣalāh is invalidated when two or more letters worth of sounds such as laughter, crying, groaning, clearing the throat, blowing, sighing, or similar are audible. If the need to cough arises involuntarily, a person should try his utmost to suppress it. However if after trying hard, the need still subsists, he may cough for relief even if a sound of two or more syllables is formed.

[64] Any action that invalidates the fast like inserting a stick into the body cavity.

[65] The ṣalāh is invalidated when any (even if a little) substance reaches the body cavity intentionally. It also invalidates the ṣalāh if it occurs absentmindedly or in ignorance of its prohibition, provided the amount of the substance is commonly acknowledged to be much, though not invalidated if it is little.

[66] The ṣalāh is invalidated by adding, even if absentmindedly, a motion that is not one of the actions of ṣalāh, provided it is both considered by *ʿurf* (common acknowledgement) to be much and uninterruptedly consecutive, such as three steps or successively moving three separate body parts – like the head and two hands, though an up-and-down motion is considered as just one – or three or more consecutive motions.

[67] Such as jumping, it invalidates the ṣalāh.

10. To intentionally add an extra physical integral of ṣalāh.[69]
11. To precede the imām in two physical integrals of ṣalāh.[70]
12. To delay with the two integrals without an excuse.[71]
13. The intention of terminating the ṣalāh by suspending its termination on a foreign action.[72]
14. By doubting its termination.[73]

---

[68] One or two slight movements do not invalidate the ṣalāh. If a person only moves a finger e.g. to scratch an itching place on the body, the ṣalāh does not break even if he moves his finger tip many times.

[69] When a person intentionally performs extra integral e.g. three sajdahs or two rukuʿs in one rakʿah.

[70] To complete two integrals before the imām does invalidates the ṣalāh. If one does so absentmindedly or in ignorance of its prohibition, it does not invalidate the ṣalāh, but the rakʿah is not counted and one must now add an additional rakʿah after the imām finishes with salām to complete the ṣalāh.

[71] Without an excuse, it is makrūh to lag behind the imām until he completed an integral, and it invalidates one's ṣalāh to lag behind the imām until he completed two integrals. If the imām bows and straightens-up while without excuse one has not yet bowed, it does not invalidate one's ṣalāh until the imām actually begins going down towards prostration and one still not bowed.

[72] To decide to break one's ṣalāh if such and such a thing happens, regardless whether the event will definitely occur during the ṣalāh or whether it may happen, such as, "I will stop if Zayd enters."

[73] Not to know whether one has terminated or not; means one hesitates in one's heart, saying, "Shall I stop intending ṣalāh or continue?" The mere thought of how it would be if one were to hesitate during the ṣalāh is of no consequence, rather the occurrence of doubt that negates one's resolve and certainty is what is considered here.

Note: Sunan Rawātib – The Sunnah ṣalāh Before and After the Farḍ ṣalāh:

The optimal numbers of these are:

- Two rak'ahs before Ṣubh ṣalāh.
- Four rak'ahs before and after Ẓuhr ṣalāh.
- Four rak'ahs before 'Asr ṣalāh.
- Two rak'ahs after Maghrīb ṣalāh.
- Two rak'ahs after 'Ishā' ṣalāh.

The *sunnah muakkadah* (emphasized sunnah) consist of ten rak'ahs:

- Two rak'ahs before Ṣubh ṣalāh.
- Two rak'ahs before and after Ẓuhr ṣalāh.
- Two rak'ahs after Maghrīb ṣalāh.
- Two rak'ahs after 'Ishā' ṣalāh.

It is recommended to pray two rak'ahs before Maghrīb ṣalāh.
The sunan of Jumu'ah are the same as for Ẓuhr ṣalāh.

Witr ṣalāh – The Final ṣalāh at Night:

The best time for Witr is after the sunnah of 'Ishā' ṣalāh, unless one intends to offer the Taḥajjud ṣalāh. Witr is a minimum of one rak'ah and the optimal is to perform eleven rak'ahs. Three rak'ahs is the minimal optimal number of rak'ah and one separates them by completing two rakʿahs with salām and then performs the final rakʿah. One recites *Sūrah al-ʿAlā* in the first rakʿah, *Sūrah al-Kāfirūn* in the second rakʿah, and *Sūrah al-Ikhlaṣ*, *Sūrah al-Falāq* and *Sūrah al-Nās* in the third rakʿah.

Tarāwīḥ ṣalāh:

It is sunnah to perform tarāwīḥ, which is twenty rakʿahs of group prayer on each night of Ramaḍān.

Ḍuḥā ṣalāh:

It is sunnah to pray the Ḍuḥā ṣalāh (midmorning prayer), which minimum of two rakʿahs, is optimum eight rakʿahs, and a maximum of twelve. One completes a pair of rakʿahs with salām.

Taḥajjud ṣalāh:

Nafl ṣalāh (superogatory prayer) at night is an emphasized sunnah, even if one can only do a little. The last part of the night is the best time to offer taḥajjud ṣalāh.

Taḥiyyat al-masjid:

It is sunnah for one who enters a masjid to greet the masjid by praying two rakʿahs each time he enters. One is no longer entitled to pray it after sitting.

فَصل : الَّذِي يَلْزَمُ فِيهِ نِيَّةُ الإِمَامَةِ أَرْبَعٌ :

(1) الْجُمُعَةُ (2) وَالـــمُعَادَةُ (3) وَالـــمَنْذُورَةُ جَمَاعَةً (4) وَالـــمُتَقَدِّمَةُ فِي

الـــمَطَرِ .

Section: The Intention of Being an Imām is Compulsory[74] in Four Conditions:

1. The Friday Prayer.[75]
2. To repeat the farḍ or nafl ṣalāh in its time hoping for reward.[76]
3. A vowed ṣalāh that is to be performed in congregation.[77]
4. A ṣalāh offered before its time due to rain.[78]

---

[74] The intention of being an imām is compulsory upon the imām during *takbīrat al-iḥrām*. As for the follower, the intention of being a follower is wājib if he intends to follow the imām even in the middle of ṣalāh besides in these four conditions in which case it is wājib for him to intend being a follower during *takbīrat al-iḥrām*.

[75] If the imām leaves out the intention of being an imām during *takbīrat al-iḥrām*, his ṣalāh will not be valid.

[76] To repeat the farḍ ṣalāh that was performed in its time or nafl ṣalāh, which was sunnah to perform in jamāʿah (except Witr ṣalāh in the month of Ramaḍān because there is no repetition for Witr). And to repeat them (once) both on their time with jamāʿah (in the entire ṣalāh) hoping for the reward of jamāʿah.

[77] If a person leaves out the intention of being an imām during *takbīrat al-iḥrām*, his ṣalāh alone is valid but he will be sinful.

[78] A group of people who are gathered because of rain and they perform *jamaʿ taqdim*, if the imām left out the intention of being an imām, his ṣalāh will not be valid.

فصل : شُرُوطُ الْقُدْوَةِ أَحَدَ عَشَرَ :

(1) أَنْ لا يَعْلَمَ بُطْلانَ صَلاةِ إِمَامِهِ بِحَدَثٍ أَوْ غَيْرِهِ (2) وَأَنْ لا يَعْتَقِدَ وُجُوبَ قَضَائِهَا عَلَيْهِ (3) وَأَنْ لا يَكُونَ مَأْمُوماً (4) وَلا أُمِّـــيًّا (5) وَأَنْ لا يَتَقَدَّمَ عَلَيْهِ فِي الـــمَوْقِفِ (6) وَأَنْ يَعْلَمَ انْتِقَالاتِ إِمَامِهِ (7) وَأَنْ يَجْتَمِعَا فِي مَسْجِدٍ أَوْ فِي ثَلاثِمائَةِ ذِرَاعٍ تَقْرِيباً (8) وَأَنْ يَنْوِيَ الْقُدْوَةَ أَوِ الـــجَمَاعَةَ (9) وَأَنْ يَتَوَافَقَ نَظْمُ صَلاتِهِمَا (10) وَأَنْ لا يُخَالِفَهُ فِي سُنَّةٍ فَاحِشَةِ الـــمُخَالَفَةِ (11) وَأَنْ يُتَابِعَهُ .

Section: The Conditions for Following an Imām[79] are Eleven:

1. The maʾmūm (follower) shouldn't know of any invalidity of the ṣalāh of his imām due to ritual impurity or anything else.[80]

[79] **Ṣalāh jamāʿah is *farḍ al-kifayah*** (communal obligation) upon all males, free persons, muqīm (non-travellers), sane individuals and those that have reached the age of puberty for the five farḍ ṣalāh and sunnah for female, such that the rite of the ṣalāh be public in a manner that the manifestation of obedience to Allah's command are evident. If held in houses where the rite of ṣalāh is not public, the obligation remains unfulfilled though a house with a sign on it is sufficient. It is best for men to offer ṣalāh in jamāʿah at the masjid and better for women to pray at home than at the masjid.

[80] It is valid for a Shāfiʿī to follow an imām of a different madhhab whenever the follower is not certain that the imām has omitted an obligatory component of ṣalāh. However, if certain that the imām has omitted one, it is not valid to follow him. The validity is based solely on **the madhhab of the follower** as to whether or not something obligatory has been omitted. Example, a Shāfiʿī followed a Hanafi imām who touched his private part. According to the madhhab of the

2. It should not be such that according to the madhhab of the ma'mūm, the ṣalāh of the imām is invalid and has to be repeated.[81]
3. The imām should not be a follower.[82]
4. Nor an illiterate person.[83]
5. The ma'mūm should not stand ahead of the imām.[84]
6. The ma'mūm should be aware of the movements of his imām.[85]
7. The imām and the ma'mūm are in the same masjid[86] or approximately 300 arm lengths apart.[87]

---

follower the wuḍū' of the imām is invalidated but not in the madhhab of the imām.

[81] It should not be such a follower following the ṣalāh of a person which will have to be repeated, like a person offering ṣalāh with tayammum because of cold, a muqīm who made tayammum in a place where normally water can be found easily or a person who does not find neither water for wuḍū' nor earth for tayammum. In these situations, the ṣalāh should be repeated, although the ṣalāh was valid according to the madhhab of the imām.

[82] It invalidates one's ṣalāh to take a ma'mūm as one's imām when the ma'mūm is concurrently praying behind an imām, though if his imām finishes with salām and the ma'mūm is still praying, he may then be taken as one's imām.

[83] A qari, one who recites Qur'ān properly, may not follow one who is unable to recite Al-Fātiḥah properly, irrespective of him being unable to recite other verses properly beside Al-Fātiḥah or not.

[84] The follower's ṣalāh is invalid if his heel is in front of the imām's. His heel should be behind the imām's heel, even if it be a little, but not more than three arms length, in which case, the merit of jamā'ah is lost.

[85] Whether by seeing the imām, or hearing his *muballigh* (the person who repeats the imām's takbīr in a loud voice so people can hear).

[86] Whenever an imām leads a follower in a masjid, the jamā'ah is valid even if they are at a distance from each other. Multiple interconnected

8. The ma'mūm intends to follow the imām or the congregation.[88]
9. The imām and the ma'mūm conform to each other in the movement of ṣalāh.[89]
10. The ma'mūm should not differ with the imām regarding those sunnahs which do not permit contradiction.[90]

---

masjid openings unto each other are considered as one masjid. So too, is the masjid's outer courtyard, even when there is a walkway between the courtyard and masjid.

[87] When the imām and ma'mūm are not in a masjid, but are in an open expanse such as a desert or large house, their jamā'ah is valid as long as the distance between them does not exceed approximately 144 meters. If they are farther apart than this, their jamā'ah is not valid.

[88] The follower intends to follow the imām whether at the *takbīrat al-iḥrām* or thereafter. If the follower neglects to do so, his ṣalāh is as if he had performed it alone. It invalidates one's ṣalāh to purposely omit the intention to follow the imām while at the same time praying behind him and following his motions by awaiting them for a long period of time. Awaiting the motion of the imām for a short period of time or performing one's own ṣalāh simultaneously with his does not invalidate it.

[89] A person who is offering a farḍ ṣalāh cannot follow a person who is offering a *salat al-kusuf* (eclipse ṣalāh). The jamā'ah is valid when (1) the imām is performing a farḍ ṣalāh and the follower is performing a nafl ṣalāh or vice versa, (2) the imām is performing the Ẓuhr and the follower is praying the ṣubh or vice versa, (3) the imām is praying while sitting and the follower is praying standing, or vice versa and, (4) the imām is performing qaḍā' ṣalāh while the follower is performing his current one or vice versa.

[90] If the imām omits a sunnah that the ma'mūm cannot add without considerably lagging behind, such as the first tashahhud, then it is unlawful for the ma'mūm to perform the missing sunnah. He must follow the imām. If he performs it anyway intentionally knowing that it is unlawful, it invalidates his ṣalāh. If the sunnah omitted by the imām can be done without much of a lag, such as *jilsat al-istirāḥah*, then the

11.The ma'mūm should follow his imām.[91]

فصل : صُوَرُ الْقُدْوَةِ تِسْعٌ :

تَصِحُّ فِي خَمْسٍ :

(1) قُدْوَةُ رَجُلٍ بِرَجُلٍ (2) وَقُدْوَةُ امْرَأَةٍ بِرَجُلٍ (3) وَقُدْوَةُ خُنْثَى بِرَجُلٍ (4)

وَقُدْوَةُ امْرَأَةٍ بِخُنْثَى (5) وَقُدْوَةُ امْرَأَةٍ بِامْرَأَةٍ .

Section: The Forms of Following the Imām are Nine:

Five of which are valid:

1. For a male to follow a male.
2. For a female to follow a male.
3. For a hermaphrodite to follow a male.
4. For a female to follow a hermaphrodite.
5. For a female to follow a female.

---

ma'mūm may add it without ceasing his participation in the jamā'ah. This also applies to when the imām omits the Qunūt in Subh ṣalāh, which the ma'mūm may perform it if he can catch up with the imām before the imām raises his head from second sajdah. If the imām raises his head before the ma'mūm makes sajdah even once and he has not intended to cease his participation in the jamā'ah, then the ma'mūm's ṣalāh is invalid.

[91] It invalidates one's ṣalāh to say *takbīrat al-iḥrām* simultaneously with the imām, or to be uncertain as to whether one did so or not. It is makrūh to perform some other part of the ṣalāh simultaneously with the imām, thereby losing the merit of jamā'ah.

وتَبْطُلُ فِي أَرْبَعٍ :

(1) قُدْوَة رَجُلٍ بِامْرَأَةٍ (2) وَقُدْوَة رَجُلٍ بِخُنْثَى (3) وَقُدْوَة خُنْثَى بِامْرَأَةٍ (4) وَقُدْوَة خُنْثَى بِخُنْثَى .

Four of which are invalid:

1. A man following a woman.
2. A man following a hermaphrodite.
3. A hermaphrodite following a woman.
4. A hermaphrodite following a hermaphrodite.

فصل : شُرُوطُ جَمْعِ التَّقْدِيمِ أَرْبَعَةٌ :

(1) الْبَدَاءَةُ بِالأُولَى (2) وَنِيَّةُ الْجَمْعِ فِيهَا (3) وَالْمُوَالاَةُ بَيْنَهُمَا (4) وَدَوَامُ الْعُذْرِ .

Section: The Conditions of Jamaʿ Taqdīm[92] are Four:

1. To begin with the first ṣalāh.[93]
2. To intend joining the ṣalāhs.[94]

---

[92] It is permissible to join Ẓuhr ṣalāh and ʿAsr ṣalāh during the time of either of them. Similarly it is permissible to join the Maghrīb ṣalāh and Isha ṣalāh, provided one joins them during a journey in which ṣalāh may be shortened or because of severe rain.

[93] If one prays the second of the two ṣalāhs before the first, then that ṣalāh is invalid and must be repeated after the first, if one still wants to join them.

3. Performing them consecutively.[95]
4. The continuity of the excuse.[96]

فصل : شُرُوطُ جَمْعِ التَّأخِيرِ اثْنَانِ :

(1) نِيَّةُ التَّأخِيرِ وَقَدْ بَقِيَ مِنْ وَقْتِ الأُولَى مَا يَسَعُهَا (2) وَدَوامُ الْعُذْرِ إِلَى تَمَامِ الثَّانِيَةِ .

Section: The Conditions of Jamaʿ Taʾkhīr are Two:

1. To have the intention of delaying a ṣalāh up-to after its time and to have this intention in its proper time.[97]
2. The remaining of the excuse until the completion of the second ṣalāh.

---

[94] That the intention to join the two ṣalāhs occurs before finishing the first, either coinciding with the *takbīrat al-iḥrām* or occurring during the ṣalāh.

[95] Not to pause at length between them.

[96] That continues until one finishes both ṣalāhs.

[97] To make the intention before the end of the first ṣalāh's time by an interval which could contain at least one rakʿah. If one neglects this intention, one has sinned, and praying the first ṣalāh during the second ṣalāh's time is considered qaḍāʾ.

فصل : شُرُوطُ الْقَصْرِ سَبْعَةٌ :

(1) أَنْ يَكُونَ سَفَرُهُ مَرْحَلَتَيْنِ (2) وَأَنْ يَكُونَ مُبَاحا (3) وَالْعِلْمُ بِجَوَازِ الْقَصْرِ

(4) وَنِيَّةُ الْقَصْرِ عِنْدَ الإِحْرَامِ (5) وَأَنْ تَكُونَ الصَّلاةُ رُبَاعِيَّةً (6) وَدَوَامُ السَّفَرِ

إِلَى تَمَامِهَا (7) وَأَنْ لا يَقْتَدِيَ بِمُتِمٍّ فِي جُزْءٍ مِنْ صَلاتِهِ .

Section: The Conditions of Qaṣr (to shorten the ṣalāh)[98] are Seven:

1. His journey should be at least two marhalahs[99] (approximately 81 kilometers one way).
2. The journey should be a permissible one in Sharīʿah.[100]
3. Knowledge of the permissibility of *qaṣr*.
4. Intention of *qaṣr* during *takbīrat al-iḥrām*.[101]
5. The ṣalāh should be a four rakʿahs ṣalāh.

---

[98] It is permissible to shorten the Ẓuhr, ʿAsr, and Isha ṣalāh to two rakʿahs each. To shorten the ṣalāh of a musāfir (except a sailor and a perpetual traveller) is more virtuous if the journey reaches three marhalahs.

[99] The journey's destination must be known. If a wife travelling with her husband or a soldier with his leader does not know the destination, they may not shorten their ṣalāh as long as they have not yet travelled the distance that permits shortening. When they have travelled it, then only may they shorten it. If they know the destination and the journey meets the condition, then they may shorten their ṣalāhs from the beginning of the journey.

[100] Travelling for a reason that is not disobedience to Allah ﷻ as there is no concession to shorten ṣalāh on such a journey.

[101] It not being valid if made after *takbīrat al-iḥrām*.

6. The continuity of travel till the completion of the two rakʿah ṣalāh.[102]
7. That he should not follow one who is performing ṣalāh completely in any portion of his ṣalāh.

[102] The ṣalāh takes place from start to finish while on the journey. If one's vehicle arrives before the ṣalāh is completed, one will have to perform the full ṣalāh.

Salat al-Jumuʿah

فصل : شُرُوطُ الْجُمُعَةِ سِتَّةٌ :

(1) أَنْ تَكُونَ كُلُّهَا فِي وَقْتِ الظُّهْرِ (2) وَأَنْ تُقَامَ فِي خِطَّةِ الْبَلَدِ (3) وَأَنْ تُصَلَّىٰ جَمَاعَةً (4) وَأَنْ يَكُونُوا أَرْبَعِينَ أَحْرَاراً ذُكُوراً بَالِغِينَ مُسْتَوْطِنِينَ (5) وَأَنْ لا تَسْبِقَهَا وَلا تُقَارِنَهَا جُمُعَةٌ فِي تِلْكَ الْبَلَدِ (6) وَأَنْ يَتَقَدَّمَهَا خُطْبَتَانِ .

Section: The Conditions of Jumuʿah[1] are Six:

1. The complete ṣalāh be performed in the time of Ẓuhr.[2]
2. It should be within a district of the town.[3]
3. To perform the ṣalāh in congregation.
4. There should be forty free males who are mature and permanent residents of the town.[4]
5. No other congregation of Jumuʿah in the same town should be offered either before it or at the same time.[5]

---

[1] To attend the ṣalāh of Jumuʿah is farḍ ʿayn. It is the most virtues of ṣalāh, and its day, Jumuʿah, is the best day of the week.

[2] If the jamāʿah commenced the Jumuʿah ṣalāh late and they doubt before commencing if they will be able to finish it within its time, then they must begin it as a Ẓuhr ṣalāh.

[3] In places where there is no hardship upon anyone to pray at one location.

[4] Permanent residents means that they live there and do not leave except when they need to. The minimum according to Imām Abū ḥanīfah *rahimahullah* is three participants besides the imām.

6. To deliver two khuṭbahs before the ṣalāh.

Note: Sunan and Adab of Jumuʿah:

- It is mustaḥab to perform a sunnah bath and makrūh not to do so before going to the Jumuʿah ṣalāh, though it may be performed anytime after dawn.
- It is also mustaḥab to clean the teeth with miswāk, trim the nails, remove body hair, eliminate offensive odours, and wear perfume and one's finest clothes (white being the best).
- To arrive early to the masjid, the best time being from dawn on.
- To come on foot in tranquility and dignity, and not to ride to the masjid unless there is an excuse.
- To sit near to the imām and to recite dhikr, Qurʾān and ṣalāh in abundance upon Nabi ﷺ.
- It is recommended to recite *Sūrah al-Kahf* and ṣalāh upon Nabi ﷺ on the night before Jumuʿah and during its day.
- It is recommended to supplicate to Allah ﷻ excessively on Jumuʿahs, seeking the moment when duʿās are answered.

---

[5] There be no other Jumuʿah ṣalāh prior to or simultaneous with the *takbīrat al-iḥrām* of the ṣalāh. That jamāʿah where the intention was made later, will have to perform Ẓuhr ṣalāh.

فصل : أَرْكَانُ الْخُطْبَتَيْنِ خَمْسَةٌ :

(1) حَمْدُ اللّــهِ فِيهِمَا (2) وَالصَّلاةُ عَلَى النَّبِيِّ ﷺ فِيهِمَا (3) وَالْوَصِيَّةُ بِالتَّقْوَى فِيهِمَا (4) وَقِرَاءَةُ آيَةٍ مِنَ الْقُرْآنِ فِي إِحْدَاهُمَا (5) وَالدُّعَاءُ لِلْمُؤْمِنِينَ وَالـــمُؤْمِنَاتِ فِي الأَخِيرَةِ .

Section: The Integrals of the Two Khuṭbahs are Five:

1. Praising Allah ﷻ in both the khuṭbahs.[6]
2. Ṣalāh upon Nabi ﷺ in both the khuṭbahs.[7]
3. Enjoining taqwa in both the khuṭbahs.[8]
4. Recitation of one verse of the Qur'ān in one of the khuṭbahs.[9]
5. To make duʿā for the believers, males and females in the second khuṭbah.[10]

---

[6] Saying "*Alhamdulillah*" (praise be to Allah) i.e. this particular utterance being prescribed.

[7] Ṣalāh upon Nabī ﷺ (Blessings on the Prophet ﷺ), which is also a prescribed utterance.

[8] Enjoining taqwa (fear of Allah ﷻ), for which a particular expression is not prescribed, it being sufficient to say, "Obey Allah".

[9] That conveys an intended meaning, such as a promise, threat, exhortation, or similar.

[10] The duʿā must be for their ākhirah (hereafter) as duʿās for this world alone do not fulfil the integral of the khuṭbah.

فصل : شُرُوطُ الْخُطْبَتَيْنِ عَشَرَةٌ :

(1) الطَّهارَةُ عَنِ الْحَدَثَيْنِ الأَصْغَرِ وَالأَكْبَرِ (2) وَالطَّهارَةُ عَنِ النَّجاسَةِ فِي الثَّوْبِ وَالْبَدَنِ وَالْمَكانِ (3) وَسَتْرُ الْعَوْرَةِ (4) وَالْقِيَامُ عَلَى الْقَادِرِ (5) وَالْجُلُوسُ بَيْنَهُمَا فَوْقَ طُمَأْنِينَةِ الصَّلاةِ (6) وَالْمُوَالاةُ بَيْنَهُمَا (7) وَالْمُوَالاةُ بَيْنَهُمَا وَبَيْنَ الصَّلاةِ (8) وَأَنْ تَكُونَ بِالْعَرَبِيَّةِ (9) وَأَنْ يَسْمَعَهَا أَرْبَعُونَ (10) وَأَنْ تَكُونَ كُلُّهَا فِي وَقْتِ الظُّهْرِ .

Section: The Conditions for Delivering the Two Khuṭbahs are Ten:

1. Purity from minor and major ritual impurities.[11]
2. Purity from impurity on the clothes, body and place.
3. Covering the ʿawrah (private parts).[12]
4. To stand; this applies to those who have the ability to.
5. To sit between the two khuṭbahs for the duration that one pauses between two postures in ṣalāh.
6. Continuity between the two khuṭbahs.

[11] If the khāṭib (speaker) breaks his wuḍū' during khutbah, the khutbah has to be repeated. But there is no harm if the khāṭib breaks his wuḍū' after delivering both the khutbahs and before performing ṣalāh.

[12] The khāṭib's ʿawrah (private parts) should be covered. However, this is not a condition for the listener (for the validity of the khutbah). Similarly, the conditions of purity, to be in the place of ṣalāh and to understand the khutbah are not conditions for the maʾmūm.

7. Continuity between the two khuṭbahs and the ṣalāh.[13]
8. The khuṭbah should be in the Arabic language.[14]
9. Forty people should hear the khuṭbah.[15]
10. It should be done in the time of Ẓuhr.

[13] The pause between these integrals should not be too long but should rather be according to the common understanding of people and not more than the shortest two rakʿahs of ṣalāh.
[14] All the integrals of the khuṭbah should be in the Arabic Language.
[15] Forty people including an imām.

Note: The Sunan of the Khuṭbah:

- The Khāṭib (speaker) stand on a *minbar* (pulpit) or a high place and that it be to the right of the *miḥrab* (prayer niche) and that the khāṭib stand on the right side of the minbar.
- The khāṭib says, "Assalāmu ʿalaykum" to those present when he enters the masjid and again when he ascends the minbar and reaches his seat there.
- The khāṭib sits until the *muadhdhīn* has completed the second adhān.
- When speaking, the khāṭib lean on a sword, bow or stick which is in his left hand. It is desirable for him to put his other hand on the minbar. If he does not have a sword or the like, he keeps his hand still by placing the right upon the left, or dropping them to his sides. He does not move them or fidget with one, as the aim is stillness and humility.
- The khāṭib face the jamāʿah during both khuṭbahs and should not turn to the right or left during the khuṭbahs, for it is a reprehensible innovation. It is desirable for the listener to face the khāṭib.

Janazah

فصل : الَّذِي يَلْزَمُ لِلْمَيِّتِ أَرْبَعُ خِصَالٍ :

(1) غُسْلُهُ (2) وَتَكْفِينُهُ (3) وَالصَّلاةُ عَلَيْهِ (4) وَدَفْنُهُ .

Section: There are Four Things Compulsory for the Preparation of the Deceased:[1]

1. To wash the deceased.[2]
2. To shroud the deceased.[3]
3. To perform ṣalāh upon the deceased.[4]
4. To bury the deceased.[5]

---

[1] For the Muslim deceased who did not die in the state of iḥrām nor as a martyr. When a person dies, it is mustaḥab (recommended) that his closest maḥram (unmarriageable kin) closes his eyes and jaws in order to make his joints flexible, gently removes his clothes and covers him with a light cloth and places something heavy on his stomach.

[2] It is mustaḥab that the one washing the deceased be trustworthy so that he can be relied on to wash the deceased completely and so forth. If he notices something good, it is sunnah to mention it, but if he notices something bad, it is unlawful to mention it as this is backbiting.

[3] It is ḥarām to look at the ʿawrah of the deceased or touch it except with a cloth. It is mustaḥab not to look at or directly touch the other parts of the body save with a cloth.

[4] It is wājib to perform ṣalāh over the deceased. However, it is ḥarām to give a bath and to offer ṣalāh upon a martyr. The obligation is fulfilled if a single Muslim male who has reached the age of *mumayyiz* (discrimination) prays over the deceased. It is recommended to perform the janazah ṣalāh (funeral prayer) in a jamāʿah (group). It is mustaḥab to pray it at a masjid and makrūh to offer the ṣalāh at a cemetery.

فصل : أَقَلُّ الْغُسْلِ تَعْمِيمُ بَدَنِهِ بِالْمَاءِ وَأَكْمَلُهُ أَنْ يَغْسِلَ سَوْأَتَيْهِ ، وَأَنْ يُزِيلَ الْقَذَرَ
مِنْ أَنْفِهِ ، وَأَنْ يُوَضِّئَهُ وَأَنْ يَدْلُكَ بِالسِّدْرِ ، وَأَنْ يَصُبَّ بِالْمَاءِ عَلَيْهِ ثَلاثًا .

Section: The **minimum** wash is to pass water over the entire body and the **best** is to wash the private organs, to remove filth from the nose, to wash the limbs of wuḍū᾽, to rub the body with lotus leaves and to pour water over the body thrice.[6]

---

[5] Then the deceased is buried obligatorily. It is best to bury him in the cemetery.

[6] It is wājib for the one washing the deceased to cover the ʿawrah of the deceased. It is sunnah that no one be present except him (one washing) and his assistant. Incense should be burned from the start of washing till the finish. It is best to wash the body under a roof, and best that cold water be used, heating it when necessary so as to remove filth that could not otherwise be removed or when the weather is cold, since the deceased suffers from it just as a living person would.

فصل : أَقَلُّ الْكَفَنِ ثَوْبٌ يَعُمُّهُ ، وَأَكْمَلُهُ لِلرَّجُلِ ثلاثُ لَفَائِفَ ، وَلِلْمَرْأَةِ قَمِيصٌ وَخِمَارٌ وَإِزَارٌ وَلِفافَتَانِ .

Section: The minimum shrouding is one cloth that covers the whole body. The perfect shroud for a male is three cloths and for a female, a shirt, a scarf, an upper garment and two cloths.[7]

[7] It is mustaḥab to scent the shroud with incense, to sprinkle on it an aromatic compound of camphor, reed perfume etc., to place cotton and perfume on the apertueres of the body such as the eyes, mouth, nostril, and ears and on places that touch the ground in prostration, and to perfume the entire body except if a person dies while in a state of iḥrām .

فصل : أَرْكَانُ صَلاةِ الْجَنَازَةِ سَبْعَةٌ :

الأَوَّلُ النِّـــيَّـــةُ **الثَّانِي** أَرْبَعُ تَكْبِيرَاتٍ **الثَّالِثُ** الْقِيَامُ عَلَى الْقَادِرِ **الرَّابِـــعُ** قِرَاءَةُ الْفَاتِحَةِ **الْـــخَامِسُ** الصَّلاةُ عَلَى النَّبِيِّ ﷺ بَعْدَ الثَّانِيَةِ **السَّادِسُ** الدُّعَاءُ لِلْمَيِّتِ بَعْدَ الثَّالِثَةِ **السَّابِعُ** السَّلامُ .

Section: The Integrals of ṣalāh Janazah (Funeral Prayer) are Seven:[8]

1. Intention.[9]
2. Four takbirs.[10]
3. To stand for those who are able.
4. Recitation of Sūrah al-Fātiḥah.[11]
5. Ṣalāh upon Nabi ﷺ after the second takbir.[12]

---

[8] The conditions of janāzah ṣalāh (funeral prayer) are the same as other ṣalāh, but in addition require: that the deceased's body has been washed before the ṣalāh and that the imām and the maʾmūm do not stand ahead of the body during the ṣalāh.

[9] It suffices that one merely intends to pray four takbīrs over the particular deceased person as a farḍ kifāyah act. The intention must coincide with the *takbīrat al-iḥrām*.

[10] One says, "*Allahu Akbar*", four times in the janāzah ṣalāh, raising one's hand to shoulder level at each one, and it is mustaḥab each time to fold the right hand over the left.

[11] After *takbīrat al-iḥrām*, it is wājib to recite Sūrah al-Fātiḥah. It is mustaḥab to recite taʿawwudh before it and "*Amin*" after it, but not to recite the "*duʿā iftitah*" or a sūrah therein.

[12] It is wājib to recite ṣalāh upon Nabī ﷺ after which it is sunnah to supplicate for the believer. It is also sunnah to recite ṣalāh upon the

6. Duʿā for the deceased after the third takbir.[13]
7. Salām.[14]

فصل : أَقَلُّ الدَّفْنِ حُفْرَةٌ تَكْتُمُ رَائِحَتَهُ وَتَحْرُسُهُ مِنَ السِّبَاعِ ، وَأَكْمَلُهُ قَامَةٌ وَبَسْطَةٌ ، وَيُوضَعُ خَدُّهُ عَلَى التُّرَابِ وَيَجِبُ تَوْجِيهُهُ إِلَى الْقِبْلَةِ .

Section: The **minimum depth** for a grave is a hole that conceals the odour of the body and protects it from animals. The **perfect depth** is the height of a man with his arms raised and fingers open, his chest should be placed on the soil, and it is wājib to make him (the deceased) face the qiblah.[15]

---

family of Rasulullah ﷺ and to say, "*Alhamdulillah*" before the ṣalāh upon Nabī ﷺ.

[13] The supplication for the deceased, the minimum being, "O Allah, forgive this deceased".

[14] Then one says, *"Assalāmu ʿalaykum"* twice, the first being wājib and the second sunnah.

[15] It is mustaḥab for the person burying the deceased: (1) to say, *"Bismillahi wa ʿala millati Rasūlillah* ﷺ", (2) to supplicate to Allah for the forgiveness of the deceased, (3) to place a block as a pillow for him and to pull-back the shroud enough to lay his cheek directly on the surface of the block and, (4) to place the deceased upon his right side.

فصل : يُنْبَشُ الـــمَيِّتُ لأَرْبَعِ خِصَالٍ :

(1) لِلْغُسْلِ إِذَا لَمْ يَتَغَيَّرْ (2) وَلِتَوْجِيهِهِ إِلَى الْقِبْلَةِ (3) وَلِلْمَالِ إِذَا دُفِنَ مَعَهُ (4) وَلِلمَرْأَةِ إِذَا دُفِنَ جَنِينُهَا مَعَهَا وَأَمْكَنَتْ حَيَاتُهُ .

Section: There are Four Factors That Permit the Exhumation of the Deceased:

1. To give a bath as long as the (body of the) deceased has not decomposed.[16]
2. To make the deceased face towards the qiblah.[17]
3. For wealth if it was buried with the deceased.[18]
4. For a woman when her foetus is buried with her and there is a possibility that it is still alive.[19]

---

[16] It is wājib to exhume a deceased who was buried without been given a bath or tayammum contrary if the deceased was buried without being shrouded. In such a case he should not be exhumed.

[17] As long as the body of the deceased has not decomposed.

[18] It is wājib to exhume a deceased even after the body of the deceased has decomposed; to take that wealth that has been buried with the deceased whether the owner demands it or not.

[19] That foetus which is six months of age or more because it is necessary to remove a living baby from the womb of the deceased before burial.

فصل : الاسْتِعَانَاتُ أَرْبَعُ خِصَالٍ :

(1) مُبَاحَةٌ (2) وَخِلافُ الأَوْلَى (3) وَمَكْرُوهَةٌ (4) وَوَاجِبَةٌ .

فَالْمُبَاحَةُ هِيَ تَقْرِيبُ الْمَاءِ **وَخِلافُ الأَوْلَى** هِيَ صَبُّ الْمَاءِ عَلَى نَحْوِ الْمُتَوَضِّيءِ **وَالْمَكْرُوهَةُ** هِيَ لِمَنْ يَغْسِلُ أَعْضَاءَهُ **وَالْوَاجِبَةُ** هِيَ لِلْمَرِيضِ عِنْدَ الْعَجْزِ .

Section: There are Four Rulings for Seeking Assistance:

1. Permissible.
2. Undesirable.
3. Makrūh (disliked).
4. Wājib (compulsory).

- **It is permissible** to ask for water to be brought close.[20]
- **It is undesirable** to ask for water to be poured towards the one making wuḍū'.[21]
- **It is makrūh** for someone else to wash the limbs.
- **It is wājib** for a sick person who is incapable.[22]

[20] For the purpose of making wuḍū'.

[21] Because this is the *'ibadah* (act of worship), it is preferable to show the humility and slavery in the 'ibadah and this is attained by doing it by oneself.

[22] It is wājib for one who is incapable to seek assistance even though by paying the normal salary for that task.

Zakah

Zakah

فصل : الأَمْوَالُ الَّتِي تَلْزَمُ فِيهَا الزَّكَاةُ سِتَّةُ أَنْوَاعٍ :

(1) النَّعَمُ (2) وَالنَّقْدَانِ (3) وَالْمُعَشَّرَاتُ (4) وَأَمْوَالُ التِّجَارَةِ وَاجِبُهَا رُبْعُ عُشْرِ قِيمَةِ عُرُوضِ التِّجَارَةِ (5) وَالرِّكَازُ (6) وَالْمَعْدِنُ.

Section: The Wealth upon Which Zakāh is Compulsory are Six Types:[1]

1. Livestock.[2]
2. Money.[3]
3. Crops.[4]

---

[1] Zakāh is wājib on every Muslim (male, female, adult or child) who has possessed a zakāh-payable amount for one lunar year.

[2] Zakāh on livestock is limited to camels, cattle, sheep and goats. Zakāh is wājib when one has owned (1) a zakāh-payable number of livestock, (2) for one lunar year and (3) has been grazing them on unowned open range pasturage for the entire year. There is no zakāh on cattle that were fed fodder or grain only even if they could have otherwise been grazed.

[3] Zakāh is wājib for anyone who has possessed the zakāh-payable amount of gold or silver for one lunar year. Niṣab, the minimum that necessitates zakāh for gold is 20 mithqals (84.8 grams), on which 2.5% is due and for silver is 200 dirhams (594 grams), on which 2.5% is due. While there is a considerable difference between the value of the gold and silver zakāh minimum, the minimum for monetary currency should correspond with that of silver, since it is more beneficial for the poor.

[4] The zakāh for crops is only on the staple types that people cultivate, dry, and store, such as wheat, barley, millet, rice etc. There is no zakāh on fruit except for raw dates and grapes. There is no zakāh on vegetables nor is there zakāh on seasonings such as cumin or coriander

4. Wealth acquired from business in which two and half percent of the value of the commodity should be discharged.[5]
5. Treasure troves.[6]
6. Mines.[7]

---

since the aim in using them is preparation of food, not nourishment. The minimal quantity on which zakāh is payable for crops is 618.8 kilograms of net dried weight, free of husks or chaff. The zakāh for crops that have been watered without effort, as by rain and the like, is 10 percent of the crop. The zakāh for crops that have been watered with effort, such as on land irrigated by ditches is 5 percent of the crop.

One is obligated to pay zakāh as soon as one possesses the zakāh-payable amount of grain, or when the ripeness and wholeness of a zakāh-payable amount of dates or grapes is apparent, otherwise, one is not obligated.

[5] Zakāh on trade goods is wājib for anyone who: (1) has possessed trade goods for a year, (2) whose value at the zakāh year's end equals or exceeds the zakāh minimum of gold or silver, (3) that the trade goods have been acquired through a transaction, or received as a gift given in return for something else, or such as an article rented from someone in order to rent them out to others at a profit, or land rented from someone in order to rent it out to others at a profit and, (4) that at the time of acquisition, the owner intended to use the goods for trade.

[6] An immediate zakāh of twenty percent is due when one finds a treasure trove that was buried in pre-Islamic time or by non-Muslims, ancient or modern, if it amounts to the zakāh minimum and the land is not owned. If such a treasure is found on owned land, it belongs to the owner of the land. If found in a masjid or street, or if it was buried in Islamic times, it is considered as a lost and found article.

[7] A zakāh of 2.5 percent is immediately due on (1) the zakāh minimum or more of gold or silver (excluding anything else such as iron, lead, crystal, emerald, or other, on which there is no zakāh), (2) extracted from a mine located on land permissible for the miner to work or owned by him, and, (3) that this amount of ore has been gathered by working at the site one time, or several times uninterrupted by abandoning or neglecting the project. The zakāh is only paid after the ore is refined into metal.

Note: The Zakāh of ʿEid al-Fiṭr:

- The zakāh of ʿEid al-Fiṭr is wājib for every free Muslim, male, female or child, provided that one has the necessary amount of food (2.036 kgs of wheat) or in money value thereof for the day of ʿEid for himself and those whom one is obliged to support, what one needs to clothe them, and in excess of one's debts and housing expenses.
- The Zakāh of ʿEid al-Fiṭr becomes wājib when the sun sets on the night before the ʿEid.
- The zakāh of ʿEid al-Fiṭr consists of 2.036 kgs of the main staple of the area in which it is given, of the kinds of crops on which zakāh is payable (if the main staple is bread, only wheat may be given).
- It is permissible to give the zakāh of ʿEid al-Fiṭr to deserving recipients anytime during Ramaḍān, though the best time is on the day of ʿEid al-Fiṭr before the ṣalāh. It is not permissible to delay giving it until after the day of the ʿEid, that is one may give it until sunset, and is a sin to delay until after this, and one must make it up.

Note: The Eight Categories of Recipients:

1. *Faqīr* (destitute) – someone who does not have wealth or earning that is sufficient for himself.
2. *Miskīn* (poor) – someone who has something to spend for his needs but it is not sufficient.
3. *ʿĀmil* – Zakāh collector.
4. *Muallafat al-qulūb* – those whose hearts are to be reconciled.
5. *Riqāb* – those slaves who are purchasing their freedom.
6. Those in debt
7. *Sabīlullah* (those fighting for Allah) – people enganged in Islāmic military operations for whom no salary has been allotted in the army roster.
8. *Ibn al-sabīl* – the traveller in need of money.

Saum

Saum

فصل : يَجِبُ صَوْمُ رَمَضَانَ بِأَحَدِ أُمُورٍ خَمْسَةٍ :

أَحَدُهَا بِكَمَالِ شَعْبَانَ ثَلاثِينَ يَوْما **وَثَانِيهَا** بِرُؤْيَةِ الْهِلالِ فِي حَقِّ مَنْ رَآهُ وَإِنْ كَانَ فَاسِقا **وَثَالِثُهَا** بِثُبُوتِهِ فِي حَقِّ مَنْ لَمْ يَرَهُ بِعَدْلِ شَهَادَةٍ **وَرَابِعُهَا** بِإِخْبَارِ عَدْلِ رِوَايَةٍ مَوْثُوقٍ بِهِ سَوَاءٌ وَقَعَ فِي الْقَلْبِ صِدْقُهُ أَمْ لا أَوْ غَيْرِ مَوْثُوقٍ بِهِ إِنْ وَقَعَ فِي الْقَلْبِ صِدْقُهُ **وَخَامِسُهَا** بِظَنِّ دُخُولِ رَمَضَانَ بِالاجْتِهَادِ فِيمَنِ اشْتَبَهَ عَلَيْهِ ذَلِكَ .

Section: Fasting of Ramaḍān Becomes Compulsory With the Attainment of One of Five Things:

1. On completion of thirty days of Shaʿban.
2. By sighting the moon for the person who sees it, even though he is a *fāsiq* (sinner).[1]
3. The testimony of a just person (non-fāsiq) for those who do not sight it.[2]

[1] For those who do not see it, it only becomes wājib when the sighting is established by the testimony of an upright witness.

[2] The testimony of a single witness that the new moon has been seen is sufficient to establish that the month of Ramaḍān has come, provided the witness is upright (male, and responsible for the duties of Islam which excludes boys who have reached the age of discernment but not puberty) and together with the decree of the ruler.

4. The informing of a just person whose information is reliable, whether the heart is inclined to it being or not, and also with the information of an unreliable source if one is inclined to it being true.
5. With the perception that Ramaḍān has commenced (this is) for that person who is doubtful of it.[3]

[3] If it is difficult to learn which month it is, for someone imprisoned or the like such as someone being held in a dark place who cannot tell night from day, or someone who does not know when Ramaḍān has come because of being in a land without habituations or people who know when it is, then such a person is obliged to reckon Ramaḍān as best as he can and to fast it. Such a fast is valid if it remains unknown as to whether the month fasted actually coincided with Ramaḍān, or if it did coincide with it, or if the month fasted occurred after it, though if the month fasted was before Ramaḍān, it is not valid.

فصل : شَرْطُ صِحَّتِهِ أَرْبَعَةُ أَشْيَاءَ :

(1) إِسْلَامٌ (2) وَعَقْلٌ (3) وَنَقَاءٌ مِنْ نَحْوِ حَيْضٍ (4) وَعِلْمٌ بِكَوْنِ الْوَقْتِ قَابِلاً لِلصَّوْمِ .

Section: The Conditions for the Validity of Fasting are Four:

1. Islām .[4]
2. Sane.
3. Purity from haiḍ (menstruation).[5]
4. Knowledge of its appropriate time.

فصل : شَرْطُ وُجُوبِهِ خَمْسَةُ أَشْيَاءَ :

(1) إِسْلَامٌ (2) وَتَكْلِيفٌ (3) وَإِطَاقَةٌ (4) وَصِحَّةٌ (5) وَإِقَامَةٌ .

---

[4] A non-Muslim will not be asked to fast nor would it be valid if he did, though he is punished in the next life for not doing so.

[5] A woman whose period ends during a day of Ramaḍān is mustaḥab to fast the rest of the day and is wājib to make-up the fast and the fast-days prior to it when missed during her period or postnatal bleeding.

Section: The Conditions for Fasting Becoming Wājib are Five:

1. Islām .
2. Mukallaf (reaching the age of puberty and sanity).[6]
3. Ability.[7]
4. Health.[8]
5. Muqīm (non traveller).[9]

فصل : أَرْكَانُهُ ثَلاثَةُ أَشْيَاءَ :

(1) نِيَّةٌ لَيْلا لِكُلِّ يَوْمٍ فِي الْفَرْضِ (2) وَتَرْكُ مُفْطِرٍ ذَاكِرا مُخْتَارا غَيْرَ جَاهِلٍ مَعْذُورٍ (3) وَصَائِمٌ .

---

[6] A child of seven is ordered to fast, and at ten is beaten for not fasting (not severely, but so to discipline the child, and not more than three blows).

[7] One is capable of bearing the fast. Someone whom fasting exhausts because of advanced years or having an illness from which he is unlikely to recover are not required to fast.

[8] The illness that permits not fasting being that which fasting would worsen, delay recovery from, or cause one considerable harm with, the same dispensation applying to someone who needs to take medicine during the day that breaks the fast and that he can not delay taking until night.

[9] It is permissible not to fast when traveling, even when the intention to fast has been made the night before, provided that the journey is at least 80.64 km one way, and that one leaves town before dawn. If one leaves after dawn, one is not entitled to omit the fast. It is preferable for travellers not to fast if fasting would harm them, though if not, then fasting is better.

Section: The Integrals of Fasting of Ramaḍān are Three:

1. To make an intention at night for each day of the farḍ (fast).
2. To refraining from intentionally doing things which break the fast, for the one who is conscious of his fast and is not ignorant.
3. The fasting person himself.

فصل :

وَيَجِبُ مَعَ الْقَضَاءِ لِلصَّوْمِ الْكَفَّارَةُ الْعُظْمَى وَالتَّعْزِيرُ عَلَى مَنْ أَفْسَدَ صَوْمَهُ فِي رَمَضَانَ يَوْماً كَامِلاً بِجِمَاعٍ تَامٍّ آثِمٍ بِهِ لِلصَّوْمِ .

وَيَجِبُ مَعَ الْقَضَاءِ الإِمْسَاكُ لِلصَّوْمِ فِي سِتَّةِ مَوَاضِعَ :

الأَوَّلُ فِي رَمَضَانَ لا فِي غَيْرِهِ عَلَى مُتَعَدٍّ بِفِطْرِهِ **وَالثَّاني** عَلَى تَارِكِ النِّيَّةِ لَيْلاً فِي الْفَرْضِ **وَالثَّالِثُ** عَلَى مَنْ تَسَحَّرَ ظَانّا بَقَاءَ اللَّيْلِ فَبَانَ خِلافُهُ **وَالرَّابِعُ** عَلَى مَنْ أَفْطَرَ ظَانّا الغُرُوبَ فَبَانَ خِلافُهُ أَيْضاً **وَالْخَامِسُ** عَلَى مَنْ بَانَ لَهُ يَوْمُ ثَلاثِينَ مِنْ شَعْبَانَ أَنَّهُ مِنْ رَمَضَانَ **وَالسَّادِسُ** عَلَى مَنْ سَبَقَهُ مَاءُ الْمُبَالَغَةِ مِنْ مَضْمَضَةٍ وَاسْتِنْشَاقٍ .

Section:

Major kaffārah (expiation) and specified punishment are compulsory, together with making-up the fast for he who breaks his fast of Ramaḍān a complete day by having complete intercourse in which he becomes sinner in his fast.[10]

There are six situations in which it is compulsory for one to abstain from things which break the fast[11] and also necessitate the making-up of that fast later.

1. Breaking his fast with a wrong act from his side in the month of Ramaḍān only.[12]
2. Upon one who omits the intention at night for the farḍ fast.
3. Upon one who has *sahur* (a meal before dawn) thinking that the night still remains, but it was not so.
4. Upon one who breaks the fast thinking that the sun has set but it was not so.[13]

---

[10] The legal occasion of the offense is the particular day of fasting, so that if it were committed on two separate days, two separate expiations would be necessary, though if it were committed twice in one day there would be only one expiation.

The expiation consist of freeing a sound Muslim slave, or if not possible, then to fast the days of two consecutive months. If this is not possible, then the expiation is to feed sixty poor persons (509 grams of food to each poor person). If one is unable to do this, the expiation remains as an unperformed obligation upon the person concerned.

The woman with whom intercourse is performed is not obliged to expiate it.

[11] Wājib to fast the remainder of the day.

[12] Like a person who is intoxicated from the night until the morning of Ramaḍān, it is binding for him to abstain from things which break the fast and also to recover that fast later.

5. Upon one who has reckoned the 30th of Sha'bān to be the first of Ramaḍān.
6. Upon one who was excessive in gargling and in putting water into the nostrils to such an extent that the water goes down the throat.[14]

فصل : يَبْطُلُ الصَّوْمُ بِرِدَّةٍ وَحَيْضٍ وَنِفَاسٍ أَوْ وِلادَةٍ وَجُنُونٍ وَلَوْ لَحْظَةً وَبِإِغْمَاءٍ وَسُكْرٍ تَعَدَّى بِهِ إِنْ عَمَّا جَمِيعَ النَّهَارِ .

Section: Fasting is nullified with apostasy, menstruation, postnatal bleeding, childbirth, insanity even for a moment, unconsciousness and unlawful intoxicants if they last for the entire day.

[13] It is best to hasten breaking the fast when one is certain that the sun has set.

[14] If some water slips down when a lot has not been used, it does not break the fast.

فصل : الإِفْطَارُ فِي رَمَضَانَ أَرْبَعَةُ أَنْوَاعٍ :

(1) وَاجِبٌ كَمَا فِي الْحَائِضِ وَالنُّفَسَاءِ (2) وَجَائِزٌ كَمَا فِي الْمُسَافِرِ وَالْمَرِيضِ

(3) وَلَا وَلَا كَمَا فِي الْمَجْنُونِ (4) وَ مُحَرَّمٌ كَمَنْ أَخَّرَ قَضَاءَ رَمَضَانَ مَعَ تَمَكُّنِهِ

حَتَّى ضَاقَ الْوَقْتُ عَنْهُ .

Section: The Breaking of the Fast in Ramaḍān are Four Types (In Respect to Rulings):

1. Wājib, like for a woman who experiences haiḍ and postnatal bleeding.
2. Permissible, like a traveller and a sick person.
3. That which is neither wājib nor permissible, like insanity.
4. Ḥarām, like he who delays the making-up of Ramaḍān despite having the capability to do so, until the time does not permit it.[15]

[15] Someone obliged to make-up some fast-days of Ramaḍān is recommended to do so consecutively and immediately. It is not permissible for a person with some unperformed fast-days of Ramaḍān to delay making them up until the next Ramaḍān unless there is an excuse for delaying.

وَأَقْسَامُ الإِفْطَارِ أَرْبَعَةٌ أَيْضا :

مَا يَلْزَمُ فِيهِ الْقَضَاءُ c وَالْفِدْيَةُ وَهُوَ اثْنَانِ **الأَوَّلُ** : الإِفْطَارُ لِخَوْفٍ عَلَى غَيْرِهِ **وَالثَّانِي** : الإِفْطَارُ مَعَ تَأْخِيرِ قَضَاءٍ مَعَ إِمْكَانِهِ حَتَّى يَأْتِيَ رَمَضَانُ آخَرُ **وَثَانِيهَا** : مَا يَلْزَمُ فِيهِ الْقَضَاءُ دُونَ الْفِدْيَةِ وَهُوَ يَكْثُرُ كَمُغْمى عَلَيْهِ **وَثَالِثُهَا** : مَا يَلْزَمُ فِيهِ الْفِدْيَةُ دُونَ الْقَضَاءُ وَهُوَ شَيْخٌ كَبِيرٌ **وَرَابِعُهَا** : لا ولا وَهُوَ الْمَجْنُونُ الَّذِي لَمْ يَتَعَدَّ بِجُنُونِهِ .

The Types of Breaking the Fast are Four:

1. The things that make qaḍā’ and fidyah[16] wājib are two:
    - Breaking the fast due to the fear of harm for others.[17]
    - Breaking the fast and thereafter delaying to make-up for it until the next Ramaḍān comes.[18]
2. Those for which qaḍā’ is compulsory but not the fidyah, like one who is unconscious.
3. Those for which fidyah is compulsory but not the qaḍā’, like a very old man.
4. That which is neither wājib nor permissible,[19] like the insane person who's insanity is not caused by transgression.

---

[16] One must pay 509 grams of food to the poor for each fast-day missed, in addition to making it up.

[17] A woman who is breast-feeding a baby or is pregnant and apprehends harm to herself or her child may omit the fast and make it up later, though if she omits it because of fear of harm for the child alone not for herself then she must give 509 grams of food in charity for each day missed as an expiation in addition to making-up each day.

[18] When making-up, if a fast-day is delayed until a second Ramaḍān comes, then one must pay an additional 509 grams to be paid for that day.

[19] A person who is forced, his fast will not break because he is not responsibled for what he has been forced to do.

فصل : الَّذِي لا يُفْطِرُ مِمَّا يَصِلُ إِلَى الْجَوْفِ سَبْعَةُ أَفْرَادٍ :

(1) مَا يَصِلُ إِلَى الْجَوْفِ بِنِسْيَانٍ (2) أَوْ جَهْلٍ (3) أَوْ إِكْرَاهٍ (4) وَبِجَرَيَانِ رِيقٍ بِمَا بَيْنَ أَسْنَانِهِ وَقَدْ عَجَزَ عَنْ مَجِّهِ لِعُذْرِهِ (5) وَمَا وَصَلَ إِلَى الْجَوْفِ وَكَانَ غُبَارَ طَرِيقٍ (6) وَمَا وَصَلَ إِلَيْهِ وَكَانَ غَرْبَلَةَ دَقِيقٍ (7) أَوْ ذُبَابًا طَائِرًا أَوْ نَحْوَهُ .

Section: The Things Which by Reaching the Stomach, Do Not Break the Fast are Seven:

1. – 3. That which reaches the body cavity[20] out of forgetfulness, ignorance or force.[21]

4. The mixing of saliva with what is between the teeth[22] and he is unable to discharge it, he is therefore excused.

5. The dust of the road which reaches to the body cavity.

6. - 7. The dust of sifted flour or flies etc. which reach the body cavity.

[20] Through an open passage-way

[21] The deliberate intake of anything besides air or saliva into the body cavity breaks the fast.

[22] Food etc. provided this is after having cleaned between them after eating, by using a toothpick or the like between them.

Hajj and ʿUmrah

Hajj and ʿUmrah.

The Conditions for Ḥajj being Wājib are Six:

1. Islām.
2. Sanity.
3. Reached puberty.
4. Free person.
5. The way towards Makkah is safe.[1]
6. Having ability (Sufficient provision and conveyance for the journey).[2]

---

[1] Safety for one's person and property from predators and enemies, whether the latter be non-Muslims or highway robbers, even when the amount is inconsiderable including ḥajj fees.

[2] To be able to pay for the provision and transportation for the journey, with money one has that is in excess of the amount one requires to support and cloth the members of one's family. This applies to one who is travelling there and back, and while obtaining lodgings for oneself, and that is in excess of any money one owes for debts, even those not yet due. It is also a condition that one have sufficient time to travel to Makkah al-Mukarramah means that one can reach Makkah and having sufficient time to perform all the rituals of ḥajj.

The Integrals of Ḥajj are Six:

1. ***Iḥrām*** – to make the intention of performing ḥajj in the heart and to recite the talbiyah.
2. ***Wuqūf*** – To stay in 'Arāfah; even if it be for a little while after zawāl of the 9th of Dhul Ḥijjah until the dawn of the 10th of Dhul Ḥijjah.
3. To make "***ṭawaf al-Ifāḍah***" which is performed after the stay in 'Arāfah.[3]
4. ***Sa'ī*** - going between ṣafā and Marwah.[4]
5. ***Ḥalq*** – shaving or shortening the hair.[5]
6. ***Tartīb*** (sequence).

The Integrals of 'Umrah are Five:

1. IḤrām – to make the intention of performing 'umrah in the heart.
2. To make ṭawaf of 'umrah.

---

[3] On the 10th Dhul ḥijjah, one enters Makkah and performs ṭawāf al-Ifāḍah, which is an integral without which the ḥajj remains unfinished (meaning that, it may not be compensated for by merely slaughtering, though the time it may be performed is anytime thereafter.).

[4] Seven times, one begins at ṣafā and ends at Marwah

[5] The best way for men is to shave the entire head, though one may confine oneself by removing, by any means, three hairs thereof from the head, not something such as the beard or moustache, or may merely shorten it, for which the optimal is to clip a little less than two centimetres from all the hair. As for women, it is optimal for them to shorten their hair in the latter way, it being makrūh (offensive) for a woman to shave her head.

3. Sa'ī - going between S□afā and Marwah.
4. Shaving or shortening the hair.
5. Tartīb (sequence).

The Wājibat (Requisites)[6] of Ḥajj are Five:

1. One enters iḥrām at the miqat (proper site).
2. Staying the night at Muzdālifah.[7]
3. Stoning the three "*al-Jamrat*" (the stoning site).
4. Staying the night following the 'Eid[8] at Mīnā.[9]
5. *ṭawāf al-wada'*

---

[6] Arkān (integrals) and wājib (requisites) are synonyms except in this chapter, the integral means that ḥajj will not exist except with it, and the requisite means the dam (expiation) becomes compulsory by leaving it.

[7] When the sun sets on 9 Dhul ḥijjah, those on ḥajj go forth to Muzdālifah occupied with dhikr and talbiyah proceeding with tranquillity and dignity, and they join the Maghrīb and 'Ishā' at Muzdālifah.

[8] *Ayyām al-tashrīq* – 11, 12, 13 of Dhul ḥijjah.

[9] When finished with the *ṭawāf al-Ifāḍah* and going between ṣafā and Marwah, [doing the latter if one had not yet previously performed it after the *ṭawāf qudūm* (arrival circumambulation)], one is obliged to return to Mina to stay overnight there and to stone on the days following the 'Eid (*Ayyām al-Tashrīq*). It is desirable to arrive before noon to perform the Ẓuhr prayer there as the Prophet ﷺ did, and to spend the night there.
One picks up twenty-one pebbles from Mīnā on the days after the 'Eid, taking care to shun the three places of stoning.

Unlawful Things While in Iḥrām are Ten:

1. Men wearing sewn garments.
2. Men covering their head.
3. Combing hair.
4. Shaving hair or plucking it.
5. Trimming nails.
6. Applying perfume.
7. Killing a game animal.
8. Performing nikāh.
9. Having sexual intercourse
10. Sexual foreplay other than intercourse.

The Expiations of Ḥajj and ʿUmrah are Four Categories:

(I) **Dam tartīb wa taqdīr** – expiation consist of alternatives in a fixed precedence order and predetermined amount:

- One must slaughter a sheep and distribute its meat to the poor in the ḥarām, or if unable to slaughter, then,
- One must fast three days during the Ḥajj and seven more at home, making ten days, or if one fails to do so while there, as is obligatory,
- They become a makeup fast that must be performed before the other seven fasted at home by an interval equal to the days of oneʿs journey home.

There are nine things which necessitate this type of expiation:

1. Performing an ʿumrah first (tamattuʿ ḥajj).
2. Performing ḥajj and ʿumrah simultaneously (qiran).
3. Not standing at ʿArāfah.
4. To miss stoning at the stoning sites of Mīnā on the three days after the ʿEid, the time for which ends at sunset on the third day if one does not leave early.
5. To miss all three nights at Mīnā after the ʿEid, though if one only misses a single night, one distributes 509 grams of wheat to the poor of the ḥarām, and if two nights, then double this amount.
6. To miss spending the night at Muzdalifah.
7. Not entering iḥrām at the mīqāt (proper site).
8. Breaking one's vow.
9. Not performing the Ṭawāf al-Wadaʿ (farewell circumambulation).

(II) **Dam takhyīr wa taqdīr** – expiation in which one is free to choose one of three predetermined alternatives namely:

- To slaughter and distribute a sheep.
- To fast three days, even if unconsecutive, wherever one wishes.

- To give 2.036 kgs of wheat to each of six of the poor of the ḥarām.

There are eight things which necessitate this type of expiation:

1. Removal of three hairs at one time and place, meaning that the interval between removing each is not considered long, and one has remained at the same place, though if their removal does not occur at a single time and place, one must pay 509 grams of wheat to the poor or fast one day for each hair, even if their number exceeds three.
2. Trimming three nails at one time and place, with the same rules and restriction as just mentioned.
3. Men wearing sewn garments or covering their head, or women covering their faces.
4. Using oil.
5. Using scent.
6. Sexual foreplay other than intercourse.
7. Having sexual intercourse a second time after having spoiled one's ḥajj by an initial sexual intercourse.
8. Having sexual intercourse between partial and full release from iḥrām.[10]

---

[10] The release from iḥrām in ḥajj is in two stages, partial and full: Partial release from iḥrām occurs when any two of the three rites of stoning, cutting the hair and ṭawāf are performed. Doing any two of them accomplishes partial release from iḥrām, rendering permissible all

(III) **Dam tartīb wa taʿdīl** – expiation in a fixed precedence order of alternatives involving estimate-based substitutes:

It is necessary due to two things:

1. Being prevented by another from completing all the integrals of the ḥajj or ʿumrah, in which case one must release oneself from iḥrām by:

- One must slaughter a sheep and distribute its meat to the poor in the ḥarām, or if unable to slaughter, then,
- One must fast three days during the ḥajj and seven more at home, making ten days, or if one fails to do so while there as is obligatory,
- They become a makeup fast that must be performed before the other seven fasted at home by an interval.

2. Having spoiled one's ḥajj or ʿumrah by sexual intercourse[11] in which case one must slaughter a camel, or if unable to,

---

things that were made unlawful by iḥrām except those relating to women, such as sexual intercourse, getting married, or touching with desire.

Full release from iḥrām occurs when all three rites have been performed, and it renders permissible everything made unlawful by iḥrām, though one still has to stone at the three jamrat and stay overnight at Mīnā during the days following the 'Eid (*Ayyām al-Tashrīq*).

[11] If one intentionally has sexual intercourse before finishing one's ʿumrah, or while on ḥajj before partial release from iḥrām. It is wājib to pay the expiation for the male, not the female.

then one must slaughter, (2) a cow, but if not possible, then, (3) seven sheep, but if not possible, then, (4) one estimates the cost of a camel and how much food this would buy, and then gives that much food to the poor in the ḥarām, but if not possible, then, (5) one fasts one day for every 509 grams of food that would have been given had (4) been done. (One may fast anywhere, but it is not permissible to delay it without an excuse.)

(IV) **Dam takhyīr wa taʿdīl** - expiation in which one is free to choose between alternatives consisting of estimate-based substitutes.

It is necessitated by two things:

1. Killing a game animal while in iḥrām, one may fulfil the expiation either by slaughtering a domestic animal that is like the wild animal which was killed, or to distribute funds to the poor, which equal the value of the game animal or to buy food equal to the animal's value and to distribute it as charity or to fast one day for each 509 grams of food. Although if the animal was a pigeon, one is obliged to slaughter a sheep which is obligatory for killing even a single pigeon.

2. Destroying a tree of the ḥarām, where, if it is large in relation to other trees of its kind, one slaughters and distributes a cow, and if small, one slaughters a sheep.

To Visit the Tomb of Rasūlullah ﷺ

It is mustaḥab when one has finished the ḥajj to visit the tomb of Rasūlullah ﷺ in al-Madīnah al-Munawwarah.

وَاللّٰــهُ أَعْلَمُ بِالصَّوَابِ.

Allah knows best.

Khatimah

نَسْأَلُ اللّٰــهَ الْكَرِيمَ بِجَاهِ نَبِيِّهِ الْوَسِيمِ أَنْ يُخْرِجَنِي مِنَ الدُّنْيَا مُسْلِما وَوَالِدَيَّ

وَأَحِبَّائِي وَمَنْ إِلَيَّ انْتَمَى وَأَنْ يَغْفِرَلِي وَلَهُمْ مُقْحَمَاتٍ وَلَـمَما وَصَلَّى اللّٰــهُ عَلَى

سَيِّدِنَا مُحَمَّدِ بْنِ عَبْدِ اللّٰــهِ بْنِ عَبْدِ الْمُطَّلِبِ بْنِ هَاشِمٍ بْنِ عَبْدِ مَنَافٍ رَسُولِ

اللّٰــهِ إِلَى كَافَّةِ الْخَلْقِ رَسُولِ الْمَلَاحِمِ حَبِيبِ اللّٰــهِ الْفَاتِحِ الْخَاتِمِ ، وَآلِهِ

وَصَحْبِهِ أَجْمَعِينَ ، وَالْحَمْدُ لِلّٰــهِ رَبِّ الْعَالَمِينَ .

تم بعون اللّٰــه تعالى متن سفينة النجاء.

We ask Almighty Allah through the dignity of His graceful prophet that He takes me, my parents, my beloved ones, and those who were related to me, from this world as Muslims, and that He forgives me and them for our recklessness and weakness. Peace be upon our master Muḥammad ibn ʿAbdullah ibn ʿAbdul Muṭṭalib ibn Hāshim ibn ʿAbd Manaf, the Messenger of Allah to the entire creation, the Warrior Prophet, the Beloved of Allah, the Conqueror and the Seal, and peace be upon his entire family and all his Companions. All praise is due to Allah, Lord of all the worlds.

The text of *"Safīnat al-najā"* (The Ship of Salvation) is complete with the help of Allah the Exalted.

Appendices

Appendix 1: Selected Duʿās and Adhkar

Duʿā for Seeking Knowledge:

اَللَّهُمَّ إِنِّي أَسْأَلُكَ عِلْماً نَافِعاً وَرِزْقاً طَيِّباً وَعَمَلاً مُتَقَبَّلاً.

Duʿā for all conditions:

اَللَّهُمَّ إِنِّي أَسْأَلُكَ العَفْوَ وَالْعَافِيَةَ ، اَللَّهُمَّ إِنِّي أَسْأَلُكَ

الهُدَى وَالتُّقَى وَالْعَفَافَ وَالْغِنَى.

Ṭahārah – Purification

Duʿā before commencing wuḍūʾ:

أَعُوذُ بِاللَّـهِ مِنَ الشَّيْطَانِ الرَّجِيمِ .

Duʿā when beginning wuḍūʾ:

بِسْمِ اللَّـهِ الرَّحْمٰنِ الرَّحِيمِ .

اَلْحَمْدُ لِلَّـهِ عَلَى الْإِسْلَامِ وَنِعْمَتِهِ ، الْحَمْدُ لِلَّـهِ الَّذِي جَعَلَ

الْمَاءَ طَهُورًا وَالْإِسْلَامَ نُورًا ، رَبِّ أَعُوذُ بِكَ مِنْ هَمَزَاتِ

الشَّيَاطِينِ وَأَعُوذُ بِكَ رَبِّ أَنْ يَحْضُرُونَ .

Duʿā after wuḍūʾ:

أَشْهَدُ أَنْ لَا إِلَهَ إِلَّا اللَّـهُ وَحْدَهُ لَا شَرِيكَ لَهُ وَأَشْهَدُ أَنَّ

مُحَمَّدًا عَبْدُهُ وَرَسُولُهُ .

اَللَّهُمَّ اجْعَلْنِي مِنَ التَّوَّابِيْنَ ، وَ اجْعَلْنِي مِنَ الْـمُتَطَهِّرِيْنَ ،

وَاجْعَلْنِي مِنْ عِبَادِكَ الصَّالِـحِيْنَ ، سُبْحَانَكَ اللَّهُمَّ

وَبِحَمْدِكَ أَشْهَدُ أَن لَّا إِلٰهَ إِلَّا أَنْتَ ، أَسْتَغْفِرُكَ ، وَأَتُوبُ

إِلَيْكَ .

Du'ā entering toilet:

بِسْمِ اللَّـهِ ، اَللَّهُمَّ إِنِّي أَعُوذُبِكَ مِنَ الْـخُبُثِ وَالْخَبَائِثِ .

Du'ā leaving toilet:

غُفْرَانَكَ الْحَمْدُ لِلَّـهِ الَّذِي أَذْهَبَ عَنِّي الْأَذَى وَعَافَانِي.

Ṣalāh – Prayer

Du'ā after adhān:

اللَّهُمَّ رَبَّ هَذِهِ الدَّعْوَةِ التَّامَّةِ وَالصَّلاَةِ الْقَائِمَةِ ، آتِ

سَيِّدَنَا مُحَمَّدًا الْوَسِيلَةَ وَالْفَضِيلَةَ وَابْعَثْهُ مَقَامًا مَحْمُودًا الَّذِي

وَعَدْتَهُ ، إِنَّكَ لاَ تُخْلِفُ الْمِيعَاد .

Du'ā Iftitah:

اللَّهُ أَكْبَرُ كَبِيرًا وَالْحَمْدُ لِلَّهِ كَثِيرًا وَسُبْحَانَ اللَّهِ بُكْرَةً

وَأَصِيلًا ، وَجَّهْت وَجْهِي لِلَّذِي فَطَرَ السَّمَاوَاتِ وَالْأَرْض

حَنِيفًا مُسْلِماً ، وَمَا أَنَا مِنْ الْمُشْرِكِينَ ، إِنَّ صَلَاتِي وَنُسُكِي

وَمَحْيَايَ وَمَمَاتِي لِلَّـهِ رَبِّ الْعَالَمِينَ ، لَا شَرِيكَ لَهُ وَبِذَٰلِكَ

أُمِرْتُ وَأَنَا مِنْ الْـمُسْلِمِينَ .

Duʿā during ruku:

سُبْحَانَ رَبِّيَ الْعَظِيمِ وَبِحَمْدِهِ (3 times)

اللَّهُمَّ لَكَ رَكَعْتُ وَبِكَ آمَنْتُ وَلَكَ أَسْلَمْتُ ، خَشَعَ لَكَ

سَمْعِي وَبَصَرِي وَمُخِّي وَعَظْمِي وَعَصَبِي وَمَا اسْتَقَلَّتْ بِهِ

قَدَمِي .

Duʿā during ʿitidal:

رَبَّنَا وَلَكَ الْحَمْدُ حَمْدًا كَثِيرًا طَيِّبًا مُبَارَكًا فِيهِ ، مِلْءَ

السَّمَوَاتِ وَمِلْءَ الْأَرْضِ وَمِلْءَ مَا شِئْتَ مِنْ شَيْءٍ بَعْدُ .

Duʿā during sitting between two sajdahs:

رَبِّ اغْفِرْ لِي وَارْحَمْنِي وَاجْبُرْنِي وَارْفَعْنِي وَارْزُقْنِي وَاهْدِنِي

وَعَافِنِي وَاعْفُ عَنِّي .

Duʿā during sajdah:

سُبْحَانَ رَبِّيَ الْأَعْلَى وَبِحَمْدِهِ (3 times)

اللَّهُمَّ لَك سَجَدْت وَبِك آمَنْت وَلَك أَسْلَمْت ، سَجَدَ

وَجْهِي لِلَّذِي خَلَقَهُ وَصَوَّرَهُ وَشَقَّ سَمْعَهُ وَبَصَرَهُ بِحَوْلِهِ

وَقُوَّتِهِ ، تَبَارَكَ اللَّهُ أَحْسَنُ الْخَالِقِينَ .

Al-Tashahhud:

التَّحِيَّاتُ الْمُبَارَكَاتُ الصَّلَوَاتُ الطَّيِّبَاتُ لِلَّـهِ ، السَّلَامُ

عَلَيْكَ أَيُّهَا النَّبِيُّ وَرَحْمَةُ اللَّـهِ وَبَرَكَاتُهُ ، السَّلَامُ عَلَيْنَا وَعَلَى

عِبَادِ اللَّـهِ الصَّالِحِينَ ، أَشْهَدُ أَنْ لَا إِلَهَ إِلَّا اللَّـهُ وَأَشْهَدُ أَنَّ

مُحَمَّدًا رَسُولُ اللَّـهِ.

Al-Salat al-Ibrahimiyyah:

اللَّهُمَّ صَلِّ عَلَى سَيِّدِنَا مُحَمَّدٍ وَعَلَى آلِ سَيِّدِنَا مُحَمَّدٍ ، كَمَا

صَلَّيْت عَلَى سَيِّدِنَا إِبْرَاهِيمَ وَعَلَى آلِ سَيِّدِنَا إِبْرَاهِيمَ ،

وَبَارِكْ عَلَى سَيِّدِنَا مُحَمَّدٍ وَعَلَى آلِ سَيِّدِنَا مُحَمَّدٍ ، كَمَا بَارَكْت

عَلَى سَيِّدِنَا إِبْرَاهِيمَ وَعَلَى آلِ سَيِّدِنَا إِبْرَاهِيمَ ، فِي الْعَالَمِينَ

إِنَّكَ حَمِيدٌ مَجِيدٌ .

Duʿā after tashahhud before salām:

اللَّهُمَّ اغْفِرْ لِي مَا قَدَّمْتُ وَمَا أَخَّرْتُ ، و مَا أَسْرَرْت وَمَا

أَعْلَنْت ، وَمَا أَسْرَفْت وَمَا أَنْتَ أَعْلَمُ بِهِ مِنِّي ، أَنْتَ الْمُقَدِّمُ

وَأَنْتَ الْمُؤَخِّرُ لَا إِلَهَ إِلَّا أَنْتَ .

اللَّهُمَّ إِنِّي ظَلَمْت نَفْسِي ظُلْمًا كَثِيرًا وَلَا يَغْفِرُ الذُّنُوبَ إِلَّا

أَنْتَ فَاغْفِرْ لِي مَغْفِرَةً مِنْ عِنْدِك وَارْحَمْنِي إِنَّكَ أَنْتَ الْغَفُورُ

الرَّحِيمُ .

Du'ā Qunūt:

اللَّهُمَّ اهْدِنِي فِيمَنْ هَدَيْتَ وَعَافِنِي فِيمَنْ عَافَيْتَ وَتَوَلَّنِي فِيمَنْ تَوَلَّيْتَ وَبَارِكْ لِي فِيمَا أَعْطَيْتَ وَقِنِي شَرَّ مَا قَضَيْتَ فَإِنَّكَ تَقْضِي وَلَا يُقْضَى عَلَيْكَ وَإِنَّهُ لَا يَذِلُّ مَنْ وَالَيْتَ وَلَا يَعِزُّ مَنْ عَادَيْتَ تَبَارَكْتَ رَبَّنَا وَتَعَالَيْتَ فَلَكَ الْحَمْدُ عَلَى مَا قَضَيْتَ أَسْتَغْفِرُكَ وَأَتُوبُ إِلَيْكَ وَصَلَّى اللَّهُ عَلَى سَيِّدِنَا مُحَمَّدٍ وَعَلَى آلِهِ وَصَحْبِهِ وَسَلَّمَ .

Duʿā and Dhikr after ṣalāh:

It is especially recommended to recite dhikr and duʿā after ṣalāh silently:

Istighfār – recite three times.

أَسْتَغْفِرُ اللَّـهَ الْعَظِيمَ .

Dhikr to be recited one times

اللَّهُمَّ أَنْتَ السَّلامُ وَمِنْك السَّلامُ تبَارَكْتَ يَا ذَا الْجَلالِ

وَالإِكْرَامِ ، اَللَّهُمَّ لَا مَانِعَ لِـمَا أَعْطَيت ، وَلا مُعْطِيَ لِ ـمَا

مَنَعْتَ، وَلا يَنْفَعُ ذَا الْجَدِّ مِنْكَ الْجَدّ .

Ayat al-kursi

اللّهُ لاَ إِلَهَ إِلاَّ هُوَ الْحَيُّ الْقَيُّومُ لاَ تَأْخُذُهُ سِنَةٌ وَلاَ نَوْمٌ لَّهُ مَا

فِي السَّمَاوَاتِ وَمَا فِي الأَرْضِ مَن ذَا الَّذِي يَشْفَعُ عِنْدَهُ إِلاَّ

بِإِذْنِهِ يَعْلَمُ مَا بَيْنَ أَيْدِيهِمْ وَمَا خَلْفَهُمْ وَلاَ يُحِيطُونَ بِشَيْءٍ

مِّنْ عِلْمِهِ إِلاَّ بِمَا شَاء وَسِعَ كُرْسِيُّهُ السَّمَاوَاتِ وَالأَرْضَ

وَلاَ يَؤُودُهُ حِفْظُهُمَا وَهُوَ الْعَلِيُّ الْعَظِيمُ ۞

Sūrah al-Ikhlās

بسم الله الرحمن الرحيم

قُلْ هُوَ اللَّهُ أَحَدٌ ۞ اللَّهُ الصَّمَدُ ۞ لَمْ يَلِدْ وَلَمْ يُولَدْ ۞ وَلَمْ
يَكُن لَّهُ كُفُوًا أَحَدٌ ۞

Sūrah al-Falaq

بسم الله الرحمن الرحيم

قُلْ أَعُوذُ بِرَبِّ الْفَلَقِ ۞ مِنْ شَرِّ مَا خَلَقَ ۞ وَمِنْ شَرِّ
غَاسِقٍ إِذَا وَقَبَ ۞ وَمِنْ شَرِّ النَّفَّاثَاتِ فِي الْعُقَدِ ۞ وَمِنْ
شَرِّ حَاسِدٍ إِذَا حَسَدَ ۞

Sūrah al-Nas

بسم الله الرحمن الرحيم

قُلْ أَعُوذُ بِرَبِّ النَّاسِ ۞ مَلِكِ النَّاسِ ۞ إِلَهِ النَّاسِ ۞ مِنْ
شَرِّ الْوَسْوَاسِ الْخَنَّاسِ ۞ الَّذِي يُوَسْوِسُ فِي صُدُورِ
النَّاسِ ۞ مِنَ الْجِنَّةِ وَالنَّاسِ ۞

Dhikr each to be recited 33 times:

سُبْحَانَ اللَّـهِ .

اَلْحَمْدُ لِلَّـهِ .

اَللَّـهُ أَكْبَرُ .

Dhikr to be recited one time:

لَا إِلٰه إِلاَّ اللَّـهُ وَحْدَهُ لَا شَرِيكَ لَهُ ، لَهُ الْـمُلْكُ وَلَهُ الْحَمْدُ

، وَهُوَ عَلَى كُلِّ شَيْءٍ قَدِيرٌ .

Prophetic Duʿā:

- اَللَّهُمَّ آتِنَا فِي الدُّنْيَا حَسَنَةً وَفِي الْآخِرَة حَسَنَةً وَقِنَا عَذَابَ النَّارِ ، اللَّهُمَّ إِنِّي أَسْأَلُكَ الْهُدَى وَالتُّقَى وَالْعَفَافَ وَالْغِنَى، اَللَّهُمَّ اغْفِرْ لِي وَارْحَـمْنِي وَاهْدِنِي وَعَافِنِي وَارْزُقْنِي ، اَللَّهُمَّ مُصَرِّفَ الْقُلُوبِ صَرِّفْ قُلُوبَنَا عَلَى طَاعَتِكَ ، اللَّهُمَّ أَعُوذُ بِكَ مِنْ جَهْدِ الْبَلَاءِ وَدَرَكِ الشَّقَاءِ وَسُوءِ الْقَضَاءِ وَشَمَاتَةِ الْأَعْدَاءِ ، اَللَّهُمَّ إِنِّي أَعُوذُ بِكَ مِنَ الْعَجْزِ وَالْكَسَلِ وَالْجُبْنِ وَالْهَرَمِ

وَالْبُخْلِ وَأَعُوذُ بِك مِنْ عَذَابِ الْقَبْرِ وَأَعُوذُ بِكَ مِنْ فِتْنَةِ الْمحْيَا وَالْممَاتِ وخَلْعِ الدِّيْنِ وَغَلَبَةِ الرِّجَالِ .

- اَللَّهُمَّ إنِّي ظَلَمْتُ نَفْسِي ظُلْمًا كَثِيرًا كَبِيرًا وَإِنَّهُ لَا يَغْفِرُ الذُّنُوبَ إلَّا أَنْتَ فَاغْفِرْ لِي مَغْفِرَةً مِنْ عِنْدِك وَارْحَمْنِي إنَّكَ أَنْتَ الْغَفُورُ الرَّحِيمُ اَللَّهُمَّ اغْفِرْ لِي خَطِيئَتِي وَإِسْرَافِي فِي أَمْرِى وَمَا أَنْتَ أَعْلَمُ بِهِ مِنِّى .
- اَللَّهُمَّ اغْفِرْ لِي جَدِّى وَهَزْلِي وَخَطَأِى وَعَمَدِي وَكُلَّ ذَلِكَ عِنْدِي اللَّهُمَّ اغْفِرْ لِي مَا قَدَّمْتُ وَمَا أَخَّرْتُ ، و مَا

أَسْرَرْت وَمَا أَنْتَ أَعْلَمُ بِهِ مِنِّي ، أَنْتَ الْـمُقَدِّمُ وَأَنْتَ الْـمُؤَخِّرُ وَأَنْتَ عَلَى كُلِّ شَيْءٍ قَدِيرٌ .

- اللَّهُمَّ إِنِّي أَعُوذُ بِكَ مِنْ شَرِّ مَا عَمِلْتُ ، وَمِنْ شَرِّ مَا لَمْ أَعْمَل اللَّهُمَّ إِنِّي أَعُوذُ بِكَ مِنْ زَوَالِ نِعْمَتِك وَتَحَوُّلِ عَافِيَتِكَ وَفَجْأَةِ نِقْمَتِكَ وَجَمِيعِ سَخَطِكَ .

- للَّهُمَّ آتِ نَفْسِي تَقْوَاهَا ، وَزَكِّهَا أَنْتَ خَيْرُ مَنْ زَكَّاهَا ، أَنْتَ وَلِيُّهَا وَمَوْلَاهَا ، اللَّهُمَّ إِنِّي أَعُوذُ بِكَ مِنْ عِلْمٍ لَا يَنْفَعْ ، وَمِنْ قَلْبٍ لَا يَخْشَعْ ، وَمِنْ نَفْسٍ لَا تَشْبَعْ وَمِنْ

دَعْوَةٍ لَا يُسْتَجَابُ لَهَا ، اللَّهُمَّ إِنِّي أَسْأَلُكَ الْهُدَى وَالسَّدَادَ.

- اَللَّهُمَّ أَصْلِحْ لِي دِينِي الَّذِى هُوَ عِصْمَةُ أَمْرِى وَأَصْلِحْ لِي دُنْيَاىَ الَّتِي فِيهَا مَعَاشِي وَأَصْلِحْ آخِرَتِي الَّتِي فِيهَا مَعَادِي وَاجْعَلِ الْحَيَوةَ زِيَادَةً لِى فِي كُلِّ خَيْرٍ وَالْمَوْتَ رَاحَةً لِي مِنْ كُلِّ شَرٍّ .

- اَللَّهُمَّ إِنِّي أَعُوذُ بِكَ مِنْ شَرِّ الْغِنَى وَالْفَقْرِ اللَّهُمَّ إِنِّي أَعُوذُ بِكَ مِنْ مُنْكِرَاتِ الْأَخْلَاقِ وَالْأَعْمَالِ وَالْأَهْوَاءِ

وَسِيءِ الْأَسْقَامِ وَمِنْ شَرِّ سَمْعِي وَبَصَرِى وَمِنْ شَرِّ لِسَانِي وَمِنْ شَرِّ قَلْبِى وَمِنَ الْخِيَانَةِ فَإِنَّهَا بِئْسَتِ الْبِطَانَةِ.

- اللَّهُمَّ اكْفِنِي بِحَلَالِك عَنْ حَرَامِك وَاغْنَنِي بِفَضْلِك عَمَّنْ سِوَاك يَا مُثَبِّتَ الْقُلُوبَ ثَبِّتْ قَلْبِى عَلَى دِينِك اَللَّهُمَّ إِنِّي أَسْأَلُكَ الْعَافِيَةَ فِي الدُّنْيَا ، وَالْآخِرَةِ اَللَّهُمَّ إِنِّي أَسْأَلُكَ مُوجِبَاتِ رَحْمَتِك وَعَزَائِمَ مَغْفِرَتِك وَالسَّلَامَةَ مِنْ كُلِّ اِثْمٍ وَالْغَنِيمَةَ مِنْ كُلِّ بِرٍّ وَالْفَوْزَ بِالْجَنَّةِ وَالنَّجَاةَ مِنَ النَّارِ .

- اللَّهُمَّ اغْفِرْ لِأُمَّةِ مُحَمَّدٍ مَغْفِرَةً عَامَّةً ، سُبْحَانَ رَبِّكَ رَبِّ الْعِزَّةِ عَمَّا يَصِفُونَ وَسَلَامٌ عَلَى الْمُرْسَلِينَ وَالْحَمْدُ لِلَّهِ رَبِّ الْعَالَمِينَ .

Duʿā Janāzah Ṣalāh – to be recited in third takbīr:

اللَّهُمَّ اغْفِرْ لَهُ وَارْحَمْهُ وَعَافِهِ وَاعْفُ عَنْهُ .

وَأَكْرِمْ نُزُلَهُ وَوَسِّعْ مَدْخَلَهُ وَاغْسِلْهُ بِالْمَاءِ وَالثَّلْجِ وَالْبَرَدِ، وَنَقِّهِ مِنْ الْخَطَايَا كَمَا يُنَقَّى الثَّوْبُ الْأَبْيَضُ مِنْ الدَّنَسِ ، وَأَبْدِلْهُ دَارًا خَيْرًا مِنْ دَارِهِ ، وَأَهْلًا خَيْرًا مِنْ أَهْلِهِ وَزَوْجًا خَيْرًا مِنْ زَوْجِهِ ، وَأَدْخِلْهُ الْجَنَّةَ وَأَعِذْهُ مِنْ عَذَابِ الْقَبْرِ وَفِتْنَتِهِ وَمِنْ عَذَابِ النَّارِ .

Takbīr to be recited on ʻEid:

اللَّهُ أَكْبَرُ اللَّـهُ أَكْبَرُ اللَّـهُ أَكْبَرُ ، لاَ إِلَهَ إِلَّا اللَّـهُ وَاللَّـهُ أَكْبَرُ ، اللَّـهُ أَكْبَرُ وَلِلَّـهِ الْحَمْدُ .

اللَّـهُ أَكْبَرُ كَبِيرًا وَالْحَمْدُ لِلَّـهِ كَثِيرًا وَسُبْحَانَ اللَّـهِ بُكْرَةً وَأَصِيلاً ، لاَ إِلَهَ إِلاَّ اللَّـهُ وَلاَ نَعْبُدُ إِلاَّ إِيَّاهُ مُخْلِصِينَ لَهُ الدِّينَ وَلَوْ كَرِهَ الْكَافِرُونَ ، لاَ إِلَهَ إِلاَّ اللَّـهُ وَحْدَهُ صَدَقَ وَعْدَهُ وَنَصَرَ عَبْدَهُ وَأَعَزَّ جُنْدَهُ وَهَزَمَ الأَحْزَابَ وَحْدَهُ لاَ إِلَهَ إِلاَّ اللَّـهُ وَاللَّـهُ أَكْبَرُ ، اَللَّـهُ أَكْبَرُ وَلِلَّـهِ الْحَمْدُ .

Sayyid al-istighfār – The Paragon Of Istighfār :

Recite Morning and Evening

اللَّهُمَّ أَنْتَ رَبِّي لا إِلَهَ إِلاَّ أَنْتَ خَلَقْتَنِي ، وأنا عَبْدُكَ وأنا

عَلَى عَهْدِكَ وَوَعْدِكَ ما اسْتَطَعْتُ ، أَعُوذُ بِكَ مِنْ شَرِّ ما

صَنَعْتُ أَبُوءُ لَكَ بِنِعْمَتِكَ عَلَيَّ وَأَبُوءُ بِذَنْبِي ، فاغْفِرْ لِي فَإِنَّهُ

لا يَغْفِرُ الذُّنُوْبَ إِلاَّ أَنْتَ .

It is sunnah to end the duʿā with ṣalāh (Salutation) and Hamd (Praise):

وَصَلَّى اللَّـهُ عَلَى سَيِّدِنَا مُحَمَّدٍ وَعَلَى آلِهِ وسَلَّمَ

وَالْحَمْدُ لِلَّـهِ رَبِّ الْعَالَمِيْنَ

Appendix 2: Authorized Books in Shāfi' ī Madhhab

The main aspect in the foundation of the madhhab is the verdict of the al-Imām. The 'Ulamā' and the books constitute the basis and source of strength of the madhhab. The 'Ulamā' explain and elaborate the original verdict of the Imām and disseminate them while the books preserve and ensure that the authentic views of the madhhab are transmitted to a later generation.

Imām al-ḥarāmain 'Abd al-Malik ibn 'Abdullah al-Juwaynī (478 H) has gathered all four main fiqh books of *al-qawl al-jadīd* (new verdict) of *al-Imām al-Shāfi'ī* (204 H) namely ***al-Umm, al-Imla', al-Mukhtaṣar*** by ***al-Imām al-Buwaiṭī*** (231 H) and ***al-Mukhtaṣar*** by ***al-Imām al-Muzānī*** (264 H) in one book entitled ***Nihāyat al-Maṭlab***.

This book of *Imām al-ḥarāmain* has been abridged three times by his student, *Hujjat al-Islām al-Imām al-Ghazālī* (505 H). The first abridgement is ***al-Basīt, al-Wasīt*** the second and finally ***al-Wajīz***. *Al-Imām al-Rāfi'ī* (623 H) summarized *al-Wajīz* and entitled it ***al-Muḥarrar***. *Al-Imām al-Rāfi'ī* also had writen a commentary of *al-Wajiz* in two books namely *Sharh al-kabir* or ***Fath al-'Aziz fi sharh al-Wajīz*** and *Sharh al-ṣaghīr*.

Al-Imām al-Nawawī (676 H) abridged *Fath al-'Aziz* in his book, ***Rauḍat al-ṭālibīn wa 'umdat al-muftiyyīn***. This was later abridged by Ibn al-Muqrī (837 H) in ***Rauḍ al-ṭalib*** and *Shaykh al-Islām Zakariyyā al-Anṣārī* (925 H) compiled a commentary on it, naming it ***Asna al-maṭālib sharh Rauḍ al-ṭālib***. Beside *ar-Rauḍ, Rauḍah al-ṭālibīn* also has been abridged by *al-Imām Aḥmad ibn ʿUmar al-Muzajjad* (930 H) in the book entitled, ***al-ʿUbab*** and *al-Imām Ibn Ḥajar al-Makkī* prepared a commentary named ***al-Īʿāb sharh al-ʿUbāb***. *Al-Sharaf al-Muqrī ṣāḥib al-Rauḍ* abridged it second time in a book entitled ***al-Irshād***. A commentary on it was prepared by *al-Imām Ibn Ḥajar al-Makkī* named ***Fath al-jawād sharh al-Irshād***.

Al-Imām al-Nawawī had abridged *al-Muharrar* and entitled it ***Minhāj al-ṭālibīn***. It was thereafter abridged by *Shaykh al-Islām Zakariyyā al-Anṣārī* in his book ***Manhaj al-ṭullab*** and he authored a commentary on it namely ***Fath al-Wahhāb bi sharḥ Manhaj al-ṭullab***. Al-Imām al-Jauharī abridged *al-Manhaj* and named it ***al-Nahj***.

Tarjīḥ (preference) in the madhhab rests upon the verdicts of al-*Shaykhayn*; *al-Imām al-Rāfiʿī* and *al-Imām al-Nawawī*. This is the unanimous view of *muhaqqiqs* (researchers) of the madhhab. If these two Imāms have a difference opinion, the verdict of *al-Imām al-Nawawī* will be given preference over the verdict of *al-Imām al-Rafiʿī*.

If the writings of *al-Imām al-Nawawī* differ, generally the the order of what will be given preference to is (1) *al-Tahqīq*, (2) *al-Majmūʿ*, (3) *al-Tanqīḥ*, (4) *al-Rauḍah*, (5) *al-Minhāj* and his *fatāwā* (legal verdicts), (7) *Sharh Muslim*, and finally (8) *Taṣḥīḥ al-Tanbīh* and its *nukāt* (marginal note). The view on which of his books are unanimous will be given preference over the view on which only a few of his books are unanimous. The view discused under its relevant chapter is given preference over that which is discussed in another chapter.

Al-Imām al-Subkī (765 H) mentioned regarding *al-Minhaj* of *al-Imām al-Nawawī*, "In this era, this book is the most excellent book for students and many scholars to understand the madhhab." There are almost one hundred commentaries of the *al-Minhāj*. It has been abridged, explained, annotated and compiled in the form of poetry. The four main commentaries of *al-Minhaj* are (1) ***Tuḥfat al-muhtāj*** by *al-Imām Aḥmad ibn ʿAlī ibn Ḥajar al-Haytamī al-Makkī* (974 H), (2) ***Nihāyat al-muhtāj ilā sharh al-Minhāj*** by *al-Imām Shams al-Dīn Muḥammad ibn Aḥmad ibn Hamzah al-Ramlī* (1004 H), (3) ***Mughnī al-muhtāj ilā maʿrifat al-maʿāni alfāẓ sharh al-Minhāj*** by *al-Imām Shams al-Dīn Muḥammad ibn Aḥmad al-Khāṭib al-Shirbīnī* (977 H) and (4) ***Kanz al-rāghibīn sharh Minhāj al-ṭālibīn*** by *al-Imām Jalāl al-Dīn Muḥammad ibn Aḥmad al-Maḥallī* (864 H).

The above mentioned books hold an authoritative position in the madhhab. However, if there is difference opinion, preference is given to ***al-Tuḥfah*** of *al-Imām Ibn Ḥajar al-*

Haytamī and ***al-Nihayah*** of *al-Imām Shams al-Dīn al-Ramlī.* Thereafter, preference is given to ***Sharh al-ṣaghīr 'alā al-Bahjah*** and then, ***Fath al-Wahhāb bi sharh Manhaj al-ṭullāb*** both by *Shaykh al-Islām Zakariyyā al-Anṣārī.* Finally, preference is given to *Sharh al-Imām al-Khāṭib al-Shirbīnī* and *Sharh al-Imām al-Maḥallī.*

Among the books of ***al-Imām Ibn Ḥajar***, the order of merit is al-*Tuḥfah, Fatḥ al-Jawād, al-Imdād,* the *fatāwā* (legal opinions) and *sharh al-'Ubāb* have the same merit, however, giving preference to the commentary is better.

The order of merit among the ***ḥawāshī*** (marginal notes) is *ḥāshiyah 'alā Sharh al-Manhaj* by *al-Imām 'Alī al-Ziyādī* (1024 H) then *Ibn Qasim al-'Abbādī* (994 H) on al-Tuḥfah, then *Shaykh 'Umairah* (957 H) marginal note on *al-Maḥallī*, then the verdict of *Shaykh 'Alī al-Shabramillisī* (1087 H) on *al-Nihāyah.* Thereafter, *Ḥāshiyah al-Halabī*, *al-Shaubarī, al-'Anānī.* Their opinions are taken if they do not differ with the original standpoint.

Despite this, deriving rulings from the book alone without studying under the 'Ulamā' is not permissible. Rasūlullah ﷺ said:

إنما العلم بالتعلم

Knowledge is acquired through
learning from the scholar.

Appendix 3: ʿAlam – Biographical Notes

Al-Imām al-Shāfiʿī

Al-Imām al-Shāfiʿī is *Muḥammad ibn Idrīs ibn al-ʿAbbās ibn ʿUthmān ibn Shafiʿ ibn al-Sāʾib ibn ʿAbdullah ibn ʿAbd Yazid ibn Hāshim ibn al-Muttalib ibn ʿAbd Manaf, Abu ʿAbdillah al-Qurashī al-Makkī al-Shāfiʿī* , the offspring of the House of the Prophet, the peerless one of the great mujtahid imāms and jurisprudent par excellence, the scrupulously pious ascetic and Friend of Allah.

He was born in Ghazza, Palestine in 150 H, the year of al-Imām Abū Hanīfah's death, and moved to Makkah at the age of two, following his father's death, where he grew up. He was early a skillful archer, then he took to learn language and poetry until he gave himself to fiqh, beginning with hadīth. He memorized the Qurʾān at age seven, then al-Imām Mālik's Muwaṭṭaʾ at age ten, at which time his teacher would deputize him to teach in his absence. At age thirteen he went to see al-Imām Mālik, who was impressed by his memory and intelligence.

al-Imām Mālik ibn Anas and al-Imām Muḥammad ibn al-Hasan al-Shaybānī were among his most prominent teachers and he took position against both of them in fiqh.

Like al-Imām Abu Hanīfah and al-Imām al-Bukhārī, he recited the entire Qur'ān each day at prayer, and twice a day in the month of Ramaḍan.

al-Imām al-Muzānī said: "I never saw one more handsome of face than al-Shāfi'ī . If he grasped his beard it would not exceed his fist." al-Imām Ibn Rahuyah described him in Makkah as wearing bright white clothes with an intensely black beard. al-Imām al-Za`farani said that when he was in Baghdad in the year 195 he dyed his beard with henna.

Abu `Ubayd al-Qasim ibn Sallam said: "If the intelligence of an entire nation was brought together he would have encompassed it." Similarly, al-Muzani said: "I have been looking into al-Shāfi'ī's Riṣalāh for fifty years, and I do not recall a single time I looked at it without learning some new benefit."

Someone criticized al-Imām Aḥmad ibn Hanbal for attending the fiqh sessions of al-Shāfi'ī and leaving the hadīth sessions of al-Imām Sufyan ibn 'Uyaynah. Imām Aḥmad replied: "Keep quiet! If you miss a hadīth with a shorter chain you can find it elsewhere with a longer chain and it will not harm you. But if you do not have the reasoning of this man [al-Shāfi'ī], I fear you will never be able to find it elsewhere."

Yūnus ibn Abī Ya'lā said: "Whenever al-Shāfi'ī went into tafsīr, it was as if he had witnessed the revelation." Aḥmad ibn

Ḥanbal also said: "Not one of the scholars of hadīth touched an inkwell nor a pen except he owed a huge debt to al-Shāfiʿī ."

Two schools of legal thought or madhāhīb are actually attributed to al-Imām al-Shāfiʿī, englobing his writings and legal opinions (fatāwā). These two schools are known in the terminology of jurists as "*al-Qadīm*" (The Old) and "*al-Jadīd*" (The New), corresponding respectively to his stays in Iraq and Egypt. The most prominent transmitters of the Qawl al-Jadīd among al-Shāfiʿī's students are al-Buwayṭī, al-Muzānī, al-Rabīʿ al-Murādī, and al-Bulqīnī, in Kitab al-Umm (The Motherbook). The most prominent transmitters of the Qawl al-Qadīm are al-Imām Aḥmad ibn Ḥanbal, al-Karābīsī, al-Zaʿfarānī, and Abū Thawr.

Al-Subkī related that the Shāfiʿī scholars considered al-Rabīʿs narration from al-Shāfiʿī sounder from the viewpoint of transmission, while they considered al-Muzānī's sounder from the viewpoint of fiqh, although both were established hadīth masters.

Al-Imām Al-Shāfiʿī is the author of some 113 works, it was nonetheless al-Shāfiʿī's hope that "people would learn this knowledge without ascribing a single letter of it to me," and as Shaykh al-Islām Zakariyyā al-Anṣārī remarked, "Allah granted his wish, for one seldom hears any position of his, save that it is ascribed to others of his school with the words, al-Rāfiʿī or al-

Nawawī or al-Zarkashī says …" and the like. He studied and taught Sacred Law in Cairo until his death at fifty-three year of age in 204 H. the end of a lifetime of service to Islām and the Muslims by one of the greatest in knowledge of the Qur'ān and Sunnah.

Imām al-ḥarāmain

Imām al-ḥarāmain (The Imām of the Two Sanctuaries) Abū Ma'ālī 'Abd al-Mālik ibn 'Abdullah ibn Yūsuf al-Juwaynī, a scholar in tenets of faith and the Imām of the Shāfi'ī school of his time, originally from Juwain (in present-day Afghanistan), born in 419 H. He was educated by his father, and after his death read his father's entire library and then took his place as teacher at Nishapur, though he was later forced to travel to Baghdad because of trouble between the Ash'aris, Mu'tazilites, and Shiites. After meeting the greatest scholar of Baghdad, he went on to Makkah, living in the Sacred Precint for four years, after which he moved to Madīnah and taught and gave fatāwā (formal legal opinions), gaining his nickname, the Imām of the Two Sanctuaries, i.e. Makkah and Madīnah.

At length he returned to Persia, where the vizier Niẓām al-Mulk, having built a first Niẓāmiyyah Academy in Baghdad for Abū Ishaq al-Shīrāzī to teach in, built a second one for Imām al-ḥarāmain at Nishapur. It was here the Imām wrote in earnest, completing his fifteen-volume "*Nihāyat al-maṭlab fi dirāyat al-madhhab*" which no one in the field of Islāmic law had ever produced the like of, as well as other works in tenet of faith, Ashʿari theology, fundamentals of Islām ic legal methodology, and Shāfiʿī law. Among his greates legacies to Islām and the Muslim was his student al-Imām al-Ghazālī, who is said to have surpassed even the Imām at the end of his life. He died in Nishapur in 478 H.

Al-Imām Abū Ishaq al-Shīrāzī

Al-Imām Abū Ishaq, Ibrāhīm ibn ʿAlī ibn Yūsuf al-Shīrāzī al-Fayruzābādī is a Shāfiʿī Imām, teacher, and debater. Born in Fayruzābād, Persia, in 393 H, he studied in Shiraz and Basra before coming to Baghdad where he displayed his genius in Sacred Law, becoming the mufti of the Muslim Ummah (Islām ic Community) of his time, the sheikh of the Niẓāmiyyah Academy which the vizier Niẓām al-Mulk built in Baghdad to accommodate al-Imām Abū Ishaq's students.

He was known for the persuasiveness with which he could urge a case in discussions, and he authored many works, among the most famous of them his two-volume *al-Muhadhdhab fī fiqh al-Imām al-Shāfiʿī* which took him fourteen years to produce, and which furnished the basic text for al-Imām al-Nawawī's *al-Majmū' Sharh al-Muhadhdhab*. He died in Baghdad in 476 H.

Al-Imām al-Ghazālī

Hujjatul Islām (Proof of Islām) Abu Hamid Muḥammad ibn Muḥammad al-Ghazālī al-Ṭūsī is the Shāfi'ī Imām and Sufi adept born in Tabiran, near Ṭūs (just north of present-day Mashhad, Iran) in 450 H. The Imām of his time, nicknamed al-Shāfi'ī the Second for his legal virtuousity, he was a brilliant intellectual who first studied jurisprudence at Ṭūs, and then travelled the Islāmic world, to Baghdad, Damascus, Jerusalem, Cairo, Alexandria, Makkah and Madīnah, taking fiqh from its master, among them Imām al-ḥarāmain al-Juwaynī, with whom he studied until the Imām's death, becoming at his hands a scholar in Shāfi'ī law, logic, tenet of faith, debate and in the rationalistic doctrines of the philosophical school of his time, which he was later called upon to refute. When Imām al-ḥarāmain died, al-Imām al-Ghazālī debated the Imāms and scholars of Baghdad in the presence of the vizier Niẓām al-Mulk, who was so impressed that he appointed him to a teaching post at the Niẓāmiyyah Academy in Baghdad, where word of his brilliance spread, and scholars journeyed to him.

His worldly success was something of a mixed blessing, and in mid-carreer, after considerable reflection, he was gripped by an intense fear for his soul and his fate in the afterlife, and he resigned from his post, travelling first to Jerusalem and then to Damascus to purify his heart by following the way of Sufism. In Damascus he lived in seclusion for some ten years, enganged in spiritual struggle and the remembrance of Allah, at the end of which he emerged to produce his masterpiece *Ihyā ʿulūm al-dīn*, the work shows how deeply al-Imām al-Ghazālī personally realized what he wrote about, and his masterly treatment of hundreds of questions dealing with the inner life that no one had previously discussed or solved is a performance of sustained excellence that shows its author's well-disciplined, legal intellect and profound appreciation of human psychology. He also wrote nearly two hundred other works, on the theory of government, Sacred Law, refutation of philosophers, tenet of faith, Sufism, Qurʾānic exegesis, scholastic theology, and bases of Islām ic jurisprudence. He died in Tabiran in 505 H.

Al-Imām al-Rāfiʿī

Abū al-Qāsim ʿAbd al-Karīm ibn Muḥammad al-Rāfiʿī of Qazvin, Persia, born in 557 H is the imām of his time in Sacred Law and Qurʾānic exegesis. He represents, with al-Imām al-Nawawī, the principle reference of the late Shāfiʿī School. His main work, a commentary on al-Imām al-Ghazālī al-Wajiz entitled *Fath al-ʿAzīz fī sharh al-Wajīz* was later to furnish the textual basis for al-Imām al-Nawawī's Minhāj al-ṭālibīn. Al-Imām Taj al-Dīn al-Subkī noted of its author, "Al-Imām al-Rāfiʿī was steeped to repletion in the sciences of Sacred Law, Qurʾānic exegesis, hadīth, and fundamentals of Islāmic legal methodology, towering above his contemporaries in the transmission of evidence, in research, guidance, and in attainment.... It was as if jurisprudence had been dead, and he revived it and spread it, raising its foundation after ignorance had killed and buried it." He authored works in Sacred Law and history, and taught Qurʾānic exegesis and hadīth in Qazvin, where the hadīth master Imām Mundhīrī was among his students. Known as a pure-hearted ascetic who followed the mystic path, al-Imām al-Nawawī observed of him that he "had a firm standing in righteous and many miracles were vouchsafed to him." He died in Qazvin in 623 H.

Al-Imām al-Nawawī

Al-Imām Muhy al-Dīn Abū Zakariyyā Yahyā ibn Sharaf al-Nawawī, born in the village of Nawa on the Horan Plain of southern Syria in 631 H. He was the imām of the later Shāfi'ī School, the scholar of his time in knowledge, piety, and abstinence, a hadīth master (hāfiẓ), biographer, lexicologist, and Sufi. When he first came to Damascus in 649 H., he memorized the text of al-Imām Abū Ishaq al-Shīrāzī; al-Tanbīh in four and a half month, then the first quarter of al-Muhadhdhab, after which he accompanied his father on ḥajj, then visited Madīnah, and then returned to Damascus, where he assiduously devoted himself to mastering the Islām ic sciences. He took Shāfi'ī Law, hadīth, tenets of faith, fundamentals of jurisprudence, Arabic and other subjects from more than twenty-two scholars of the time, including Abū Ibrāhīm Ishaq al-Maghrībī, 'Abd al-Rahman ibn Qudāmah al-Maqdisī, and others, at a period of his life in which, as al-Imām al-Dhahabī notes, "his dedication to learning, night and day, became proverbial." Spending all his time in either worship or gaining Sacred Knowledge, he took some twelve lessons a day, only dozed off in the night at moments when sleep overcame him, and drilled himself on the lessons he learned by heart while walking along the street. Fastidious in detail and deep in understanding of the subjects he thus mastered. He authored many great works in Shāfiʿī jurisprudence, hadīth, history, and legal opinion, among the best known of which are his *Minhāj al-ṭālibīn*, which has become a main reference for the Shāfiʿī School, *Riyāḍ al-ṣālihīn* and *Kitab al-adhkār* in hadīth, and his eighteen-volume *Sharh Ṣahīh Muslim*.

He lived simply, and it is related that his entire wardrobe consisted of a turban and an ankle-length shirt with a single button at the collar. After a residence in Damascus of twenty-seven years, he returned the books he had borrowed from charitable endowments, bade his friends farewell, visited the graves of his Shaykhs who had died, and departed, going first to Jerusalem and then to his native Nawa, where he became ill at his father's home and died at forty-four years of age in 676 H, young in years but great in benefit to Islām and the Muslims.

Shaykh al-Islām Zakariyyā al-Anṣārī

Shaykh al-Islām Abū Yahya Zakariyya ibn Muḥammad ibn Aḥmad al-Anṣārī, born in Sanika, Egypt, in 823 H, is known as the shaykh of shaykhs. He was the Shāfiʿī scholar of his time, a hadīth master (hāfiẓ), judge and Qurʾānic exegete. He was educated in Cairo in circumstances of such poverty that he used to have to leave the mosque by night to look for watermelon rinds, which he would wash and eat.

When his knowledge later won him fame and recognition, he was to receive so many gifts that his income before his appointment to the judiciary amounted to nearly three thousand dirhams a day, which he spent to gather books, teach and give financial help to the students who studied with him. When Sultan Quytubay al-Jurkasi appointed him as head of the judiciary in Cairo, he accepted the post with reluctance after being repeatedly asked, but when the sultan later committed a wrong act and he sent him a letter upbraiding him, the sultan dismissed him and he returned to teaching. He authored works in Sacred Law, the sciences of Qur'ān and hadīth, logic, Arabic, fundamentals of jurisprudence, and Sufism, and was the Shaykh of al-Imām Ibn Ḥajar Haytamī. He died in 926 H at one hundred years of age.

Al-Imām Ibn Ḥajar al-Haytamī

Shihab al-Dīn Abū al-ʿAbbās Aḥmad ibn Muḥammad ibn ʿAlī ibn Hajar al-Haytamī al-Makkī is born in 909 H in Abū Haytam, western Egypt. He was the Shāfiʿī Imām of his time, a brilliant scholar of in-depth applications of Sacred Law, and with al-Imām Aḥmad al-Ramlī, represents the foremost resource for fatwa (legal apinion) for the entire late Shāfiʿī School. He was educated at al-Azhar, but later moved to Makkah, where he authored major works in Shāfiʿī jurisprudence, hadīth, tenets of faith, education, hadīth commentary, and formal legal opinion. His most famous works include *Tuhfah al-muḥtāj bi sharh al-Minhāj,* a commentary on al-Imām al-Nawawī's *Minhāj al-ṭālibīn* whose ten volumes represent a high point in Shāfi'ī scholarship; the four volume *al-Fatāwā al-kubrā al-fiqhiyyah*; and *al-Zawājir 'an iqtirāf al-kabā'ir,* which with its detailed presentation of Qur'ān and Hadīth evidence and masterful legal inferences, remains unique among Muslim works dealing with taqwa (godfearingness) and is even recognized by Hanafi scholars like al-Imām Ibn 'Ābidīn as a source of authoritative legal texts valid in their own school. After a lifetime of outstanding scholarship, the Imām died and was buried in Makkah in 974 H.

Al-Imām Muḥammad al-Shirbīnī al-Khāṭib

Shams al-Din Muḥammad ibn Aḥmad al-Shirbīnī al-Khāṭib of Cairo is a Shāfi'ī Imām and Qur'ānic exegete of knowledge and piety, he studied in Cairo under al-Imām Aḥmad al-Ramlī, as well as Nur al-Dīn al-Maḥallī, Aḥmad Burullusi and others, who authorized him to give formal legal opinion and instruction. He educated a multitude of scholars and his works won recognition in their author's lifetime for their outstanding clarity and reliability, among the most famous of them his four-volume

Mughnī al-muḥtaj ilā ma'rifat ma'ānī alfāz al-Minhāj, a commentary on al-Imām al-Nawawī's Minhāj al-ṭālibīn, and his Qur'ānic exegesis *al-Sirāj al-munīr fi al-i'āna 'alā ma'rifa ba'd kalām Rabbina al-Hakīm al-Khabīr*. He died in Cairo in 977 H.

Bibliography

Books of Fiqh:

- **Matn Safīnat al-najā᾿ fī uṣūl al-dīn wa al-fiqh**, al-Shaykh Ibn Samīr al-Haḍramī, Dar al-fikr.
- **Kāshifat al-sajā᾿ sharh Safīnat al-najā᾿**, al-Shaykh Muḥammad al-Nawawī, Dar ihya al-kutub al-ʿArabiyyah, Indonesia.
- **Reliance of the Traveller**, al-Shaykh Nuh Ha Mim Keller, Aamna Publisher, Revised Edition, Delhi, India.
- **Nail al-rajā᾿ bi sharh Safīnat al-najā᾿**, Sayyid Aḥmad ibn ʿUmar al-Shaṭirī, Second edition 2007, Dar al-minhāj, Beirut.
- **Al-Fiqh al-manhaji ʿalā madhhab al-Imām al-Shāfiʿī**, Dr. Mustafa al-Khīn, Eighth edition 2007, Dar al-Qalam, Dimashq.
- **Tuḥfat al-muḥtāj**, Shihāb al-dīn Abū al-ʿAbbās Aḥmad ibn Muḥammad ibn ʿAlī ibn Ḥajar al-Haytamī, Maktabah al-thaqafah al-dīniyyah.
- **Nihāyat al-muḥtāj ilā sharh al-Minhāj,** Shams al-dīn Muḥammad ibn Abī al-ʿAbbās Aḥmad ibn Hamzah ibn Shihāb al-dīn al-Ramlī, 1994, Dar al-kutub al-ʿilmiyyah, Beirut.
- **Minhāj al-ṭālibīn**, al-Imām Muhyid al-Dīn Abū Zakariyyā Yahyā ibn Sharaf al-Nawawī, edited by Dr. Aḥmad ibn ʿAbd

al-ʿAzīz al-Ḥaddād, Second Edition, 2005, Dar al-Bashāʾir al-Islāmiyyah, Beirut.

- **Al-Majmūʿ**, al-Imām Muhyi al-Dīn Abū Zakariyyā Yahyā ibn Sharaf al-Nawawī, First Edition 2002, Dar ihyā al-turath al-ʿArabī, Beirut.
- **Ḥāshiyatan – Qalyūbī and ʿĀmīrah ʿalā sharh Jalāl al-Dīn al-Maḥallī ʿalā sharh al-Minhāj**, first edition, 1998, Dar al-Fikr, Beirut.
- **Fatḥ al-Wahhāb sharh Manhaj al-ṭullāb**, Shaykh al-Islām Abū Yahyā Zakariyyā al-Anṣārī, Dar al-fikr.
- **Al-Iqnāʿ fī ḥalli alfāẓ Abī Shujāʿ**, al-Shaykh Muḥammad Shirbīnī Khāṭib, 2001, Dar al-fikr, Beirut.
- **Ḥāshiyah iʿānat al-ṭālibīn**, al-Imām Abū Bakr ibn Muḥammad Shatta al-Dimyātī, 2002, Dar al-fikr, Beirut.
- **Tuḥfatul Ikhwān**, Mawlānā Muḥammad Ibrahim Ba'kathah translated by Shaykh Yousuf Abdullah Karaan, Second edition 2002, Adam Publisher and Distributor, New Delhi.
- **Al-Maqādir al-sharʿiyyah wa al-ahkām al-fiqhiyyah al-mutaʿalliqah bihā kayl, wazn, miqyās, mundhu ʿahdi al-Nabi ﷺ wa taqwīmiha bi al-muʿāṣir,** Dr. Muḥammad Najm al-Dīn al-Kurdī, Second edition 2005, Cairo.

Books of Usul al-din

- **Ḥāshiyat al-Imām al-Baijūrī ʿalā Jauharat al-tauhīd,** edited by Dr. ʿAlī Jumʿah Muḥammad al-Shāfiʿī , First edition 2002, al-Qahirah.

Books of Introduction to the Madhhab:

- **Madkhāl ilā kutub al-fiqh al-Shāfiʿī, Khazain al-saniyyah**, Shaykh ʿAbd al-Qadir ibn ʿAbd al-Muttalib al-Mindili al-Andunisi, First Edition 2004, Muassasah al-Riṣalāh, Beirut.
- **Al-Madkhāl ilā dirāsat al-madhhab al-fiqhiyyah**, Dr. ʿAlī Jumuʿah, First Edition 2004, Dar al-Salām, Cairo.
- **Al-Fawāʾid al-Makkiyyah**

Books of Usul al-fiqh:

- **Sharh al-Waraqāt li Imām al-ḥarāmain al-Juwainī**, al-Imām ʿAbd ar-Rahman ibn Ibrāhīm al-Fazarī Ibn al-Firkāh, edited by Sarah Shāfi al-Ḥajirī, first edition 2002, Dar al-Bashāʾir al-Islāmiyyah.

- **Al-Wajīz fī uṣūl al-tashrī'i al-Islāmī**, Dr. Muḥammad Hasan Hītū, First Edition 2006, Muassasah al-Riṣalāh, Beirut.
- **Al-Lumā' fī uṣūl al-fiqh,** Imām Abū Ishaq al-Shīrāzī, Dar al-kalimah.

Notes

Notes

Made in the USA
Middletown, DE
18 October 2023

41023367R00104